GREAT THEMES
OF THE NEW TESTAMENT

Also by William Barclay in this series

The Apostles' Creed
At the Last Trumpet
Discovering Jesus
Good Tidings of Great Joy
Growing in Christian Faith
Letters to the Seven Churches
The Lord is My Shepherd
The Lord's Prayer
The Lord's Supper
Many Witnesses, One Lord
The New Testament
New Testament Words
The Parables of Jesus
The Promise of the Spirit
The Ten Commandments
We Have Seen the Lord!

Great Themes of the New Testament

William Barclay

Westminster John Knox Press
LOUISVILLE
LONDON • LEIDEN

Published in the U.S.A. in 2001 by
Westminster John Knox Press
Louisville, Kentucky

Original edition published in English under the title
Great Themes of the New Testament by John Hunt Publishing Ltd.,
46a West Street, New Alresford, Hants, UK.

PRINTED IN HONG KONG/CHINA

01 02 03 04 05 06 07 08 09 10 — 10 9 8 7 6 5 4 3 2 1

Library of Congress Cataloging-in-Publication Data
Barclay, William, 1907-1978.
 Great themes of the New Testament / William Barclay.
  p. cm.
 Originally published: Philadelphia : Westminister Press, c1979.
 ISBN 0-664-22385-0 (alk. paper)
 1. Bible. N.T.--Criticism, interpretation, etc. I. Title.

 BT2361.3.B37 2001
 225'.6--dc2l

                                                    00-065478

Contents

	Preface	vii
	Introduction: The Aim of these Studies	viii
1	Philippians 2.1-11: An Appeal to Christian Unity	1
2	John 1.1-14: Fully Man and Fully God	23
3	Romans 5.12-21: Sin and Salvation	45
4	Acts 2.14-40: The First Christian Sermon	67
5	Revelation 13: The Mystery of the Beast	89
6	Matthew 24: The Mysterious Prediction	115

Preface

Often a preacher finds commentaries disappointing. Like Studdert Kennedy's psychologist, they 'take the saints to pieces and label all the parts', but somehow they have 'one small weakness', they 'cannot make a saint'. William Barclay was never like this. Despite his wide scholarship and deep knowledge of the ancient world and the writings of other scholars, he always wrote plainly and positively.

In this volume he takes four of the greatest passages in the New Testament, and two slightly strange ones, and, in his own words, 'sets down what he thinks that passage first meant and what it now means'. Both tasks are important. The Bible can speak to us only if we understand what the writers themselves said; but the message is barren unless it is related to our own situation.

With his uncanny knack of picking out key points in such a way that the reader can grasp the main thrust of the passage, the preacher can find ready-made sermon outlines and a wealth of ideas.

CYRIL S. RODD

Introduction
The Aim of these Studies

Before beginning this series of expositions of great passages of the New Testament, I wish to set down the aim with which I have embarked upon it. A. B. Bruce, writing on the same passage with which we are to deal in the first chapter, said: 'The diversity of opinion prevailing among interpreters is enough to fill the student with despair, and to afflict him with intellectual paralysis' (*Humiliation of Christ*, 8). The trouble with full-size commentaries is that they frequently spend much time in two activities. They labor to set out every possible interpretation of the passage with which they are dealing, and they offer so many alternatives that at the end they leave the seeker more bewildered than when he began. And they spend much time and labor and erudition on justifying by many an argument, sometimes polemically, the view they themselves take. This is not to belittle the great commentaries; the information they supply is essential for all scholarly work. Even if one wished to, one who has spent the greater part of his working life studying them could not empty his mind of what he has learned from them, nor rid himself of the debt he owes to them. But, even so, I think that there is a place for a kind of exposition which is not concerned to state all the possible alternatives, and which is still less concerned with arguments to prove itself right and others in error, but which simply brings to a passage such equipment as it possesses, and sets down what it thinks that passage first meant, and what it now means. That is what in this series I wish to try to do; and I begin by turning our thoughts to a passage which is one of the highlights of the letters of Paul, to Philippians 2.1-11.

1
Philippians 2.1-11:
An Appeal to Christian Unity

When Paul wrote the letter to the Philippians, he was in prison, most probably in Rome (1.13, 14, 16, 4.22). To no Church was Paul closer in heart and soul than to the Church at Philippi. He yearned for them as a lover for his loved one (1.8). They are in his heart (1.7). He was praying for them, and he knew that they were praying for him (1.3,19). Nothing could delight them more than that he should be enabled to visit them again (1.26), and indeed he hoped that such a visit would soon be possible (2.24). They are his 'dearly beloved,' his 'joy and crown' (4.1).

And yet, as he writes, Paul is worried. It may be, he feels, that they will think that the imprisonment which has come to him is the end (1.12-19). He feels that they still need him and still need what he can give them and what he can do for them (1.24, 25), however much he would like to lay down his burden and to rest. They have to go through their own suffering for Christ (1.28-30). There are Jewish teachers who might well mislead them (3.18,19). And there are always earthbound creatures, who are a discredit to the Church, and who are liable to forget that they are a colony of heaven upon earth (3.18-20). So Paul writes to them, and there are three reasons for his writing.

Why Paul writes to the Philippians
1. When the Philippians had sent their gift to Paul, they had sent Epaphroditus with it. They had intended that Epaphroditus should stay to serve Paul in prison, but he had fallen ill, and had

come close to death. Perhaps Epaphroditus was home-sick; and certainly he was worried because he knew that the people in Philippi were worried about him. So Epaphroditus had to go home; and Paul writes him what is almost an affectionate testimonial. There were those in Philippi who might well regard Epaphroditus as a quitter, and Paul, with his perfect courtesy and consideration, writes about Epaphroditus in a way that will make it easy for him to go back (2.25-30). There is something very touching in the picture of Paul facing death, and yet concerned to see that Epaphroditus is not undervalued or misunderstood.

2. Philippians is a letter of thanks. The Philippians, as they had done before, had sent Paul a gift, and Paul writes to thank them for their kindly thought (4.10-18). The correspondence of Paul teaches us the courtesy which never forgets the letter of thanks.

3. But that which moved Paul to his most moving and eloquent appeal was the fact that there was danger of dissension within the Philippian Church. He beseeches them to stand fast in one spirit, with one mind striving together for the faith of the gospel (1.27). He insists that all things must be done without murmurings and disputings (2.14). He knows well how it is a human tendency for people to seek their own and not the things of Christ (2.21). The Jewish invaders may well cause a split in the Church (3.2). Euodia and Syntyche are at variance, and it would not be the first time that a personal quarrel disrupted the whole structure of a Church (4.2). The trouble at Philippi had not yet reached serious proportions but Paul was wise to the truth that prevention is better than cure, and that, as some one has put it, it is wiser to fence a dangerous road to keep people from falling over a precipice, than it is to keep an ambulance waiting at the bottom to clear up the wreckage after they have fallen over. So Paul in our passage brings every appeal to bear on the Philippians to live in unity together (2.1-11). How, then, does Paul make his appeal?

The Ideal of Christian Unity

He sets before the Philippians the ideal of Christian unity in a series of vivid phrases.

(*a*) 'Like-minded' and 'of one mind'

He uses two very similar phrases. As the A.V. has it, he urges them to be 'like-minded' and to be 'of one mind.' In the first instance the Greek is *to auto phronein*; in the second it is *to hen phronein*. The word *phronein* is sometimes translated 'to think'; but the real characteristic of it is that it describes a man's whole attitude and disposition of mind. It does not describe one piece of thinking; it describes that attitude of mind which is behind all a man's thinking. *To tēs sarkos phronein* is to have a flesh-dominated attitude of mind (Romans 8.5). *Hupsēla phronein* is to be lofty-minded (Romans 11.20). *Ta epigeia phronein* is to have an earth-bound mind (Philippians 3.19). *Ta anō phronein* is to have a mind that is set on the things that are above, as *ta epi tēs gēs phronein* is to have a mind that is interested in nothing but the things on this earth (Colossians 3.2). *To auto phronein* is literally 'to think the same'; that is to say, it is to have a mind whose disposition is harmony. It is all too true that there are people whose disposition is to make disharmony; they are characteristically disposed to look for occasions through which argument and difference may be fomented; and it is equally and blessedly true that there are those whose characteristic disposition is harmony. Paul has no doubt in which the Spirit of Christ dwells. What is the difference between this phrase *to auto phronein* and the very similar phrase *to hen phronein*? *To hen phronein* is literally 'to think the one thing.' There is no general agreement amongst commentators as to where the difference lies, and there are, indeed, many who think that there is no discernible difference, or certainly no expressible difference. I suggest that the difference may well be this. *To auto phronein* describes the general disposition of harmony which should be the background against which the whole Christian fellowship moves, and the atmosphere in which the life of the Christian fellowship is lived. *To hen phronein* describes the atmosphere when that all pervading atmosphere of harmony is brought to bear on one particular issue and one particular decision. To Paul the Christian ideal is a disposition to harmony in all things, and a situation in which that Christian harmony is the deciding influence in any time of decision in thought or in action.

(*b*) 'The same love'

Paul pleads with the Philippians to have the same love. The word for love is *agapē*. Herein lies the essence of the Christian ethic. Greek possesses four words for 'love.' There is *erōs*, which is the love of passion, and in which there is always sex. So nearly does that word become 'lust' that it never occurs in the New Testament at all. There is *storgē* which is the word for family love, the love of parent for child, and child for parent. There is *philia* which is warm, affectionate love, including both spiritual and physical fellowship and intimacy. And there is *agapē*, which is hardly a word of classical and secular Greek at all. It is a word, as R. C. Trench says, 'born within the bosom of revealed religion'. What is its essential flavor? Its essential flavor is to be found in Jesus' words in Matthew 5.43-48. There Christians are bidden to love even their enemies. Why? Because such a love is like the love of God. What, then, is the great characteristic of the love of God! God makes his sun to rise on the evil and on the good, and sends rain on the just and the unjust (Matthew 5.45). That is to say, there is in God an unconquerable benevolence. Let a man be the friend of God or the enemy of God, God's benevolence extends to him. The essential fact about this Christian *agapē* is that it is the exercise of a man's total personality. Love in the ordinary sense of the term is an emotional experience. We love because we cannot help it. As it has been said, we admire people for reasons, we love people without reason. Liking is an inexplicable thing; it happens with no effort of our own. But *agapē* is not only a thing of the heart; it is also a thing of the will. It is not a mere happening; it is a conquest. It is something into which we must will ourselves, and can only will ourselves through the Spirit of Jesus Christ. Further, this is a new thing. Plutarch's definition of a real man was that he was a man who was useful to his friends and dangerous to his enemies. The demand of Christianity is a universal and unconquerable benevolence to all people, no matter what their attitude to us, and their treatment of us is. Paul's injunction is that the Philippians should 'have the same love.' That is to say, that in the heart of each and all of them there should be this benevolence which nothing could ever sour. It is easy to see what unity such love could bring into any Church.

(*c*) 'Of one accord'
Paul urges the Philippians, as the A.V. has it, to be 'of one accord' The Greek is *sumpsuchoi* which is a vivid word. The *sum* part of the word means 'together'; and the *psuchoi* part is from *psuchē*. What, then is the *psuchē*? The word *psuchē* occurs thirteen times in Paul's Epistles. Once in I Thessalonians 5.23 we get together the three parts of man – body, soul, and spirit. The soul is the *psuchē*. But here we must have a care. The body is the physical part of man. The spirit is that part of man which makes him able to reason and to think, and which makes him kin to God; it is through his spirit that man can receive a message from God, and can enter into fellowship with God who is spirit. But in Greek psychology the *psuchē*, the soul, is the principle of physical life. Spirit (*pneuma*) is peculiar to man; he alone possesses it. But he shares *psuchē* with everything that has life. An animal has

psuchē; even a plant, insofar as it is a living organism, has *psuchē*; for *psuchē* is the life principle of everything that lives and breathes. With the exception of Ephesians 6.6 and Colossians 3.23, where *psuchē* approximates much more to the English sense of 'heart', in the meaning of the seat of the emotions and the desires, *psuchē* in Paul is the essential life principle. So, then, when Paul says that Christians must be *sumpsuchoi* he means that they must share the same life principle. They must be so united that they actually share the same life; and that becomes possible because the common life of the Christian is Christ. The unity of Christians is such that they share the one life principle; they are one in that essential life by which men live.

Things to be eradicated
(*a*) 'Strife'

Paul then goes on to tell of the things which must be eradicated. Nothing must be done 'through strife.' The word for strife is *eritheia*. It is a word with a strange history. An *erithos* was originally a 'day-laborer' and *eritheia* was work done by such a man. With such work there is obviously nothing whatever wrong. But such work is inevitably done for pay; it is done with the purpose of making a living. Then there comes into the word a change of accent and of emphasis. *Eritheia* comes to mean work which is done for no other motive than that of pay; it comes to describe the spirit of the workman who has no other interest than the pay he receives for his work. Then the word takes a final downward step. It enters the world of municipal and national politics; and it describes the spirit of the man who is actuated by no other motive than the motive of ambition: he has no conception of the service of the community; he has no idea of contributing to the public good. His one aim in seeking office in whatever society he may happen to be is his own honor, his own prestige, his own prominence and his own gain.

Eritheia is selfish and factious ambition. Chrysostom has an eloquent passage in his homily on these verses, as he warns men against *eritheia*. 'This, as I always say, is the consequence of all evil. Hence come fightings and contentions. Hence come envyings and strifes. Hence it is that love waxes cold, when we love the praise of men, when we are slaves to the honor that is paid by the many, for it is not possible for a man to be the slave of praise, and to be a true servant of God' (Chrysostom, *Homilies on Philippians*, 5). There are many people whose service in the church is absolutely selfless; but there are some few whose motive is their prestige; and there are some few in the Church and in every voluntary organization whose motive, if they knew their own hearts, is that the church and the voluntary organization are for them the only spheres in which it is possible for them to achieve a brief authority. Those who are inspired by *eritheia* are wreckers of Christian fellowship.

(*b*) 'Vainglory'
What the A.V. calls 'vainglory' must be banished from the Christian fellowship. The word is *kenodoxia*, literally 'empty opinion.' Suidas defines it as 'any vain thinking about oneself.' *Kenodoxia* is that conceit which is founded on a false view of oneself. There is such a thing as a just and legitimate knowledge of one's own abilities and talents; but *kenodoxia* is the mental attitude of the man whose whole thinking about himself is wishful thinking, who sees himself through rose-colored spectacles, who has surrounded himself with a certain romantic glamor. The one safe-guard against *kenodoxia* is an honest comparison of ourselves with Jesus Christ.

Further Virtues
(*a*) 'Lowliness of mind'
Now Paul ceases to deal in negatives and comes back to

positives again. The Christian must live in 'lowliness of mind.'
The word is *tapeinophrosunē*. This is a distinctively Christian
word. It is a commonplace to note that in classical Greek there
is no word for 'humility' which has not some tinge of that which
is mean, ungenerous and low. *Tapeinophrosunē* is what Vincent
called 'an out-growth of the gospel,' and what Trench called 'a
birth of the gospel.' In the New Testament the word occurs in
seven other passages besides this passage. Once it refers to
man's attitude to God and to the attitude of the service which is
worship (Acts 20.19). Twice it is used of a false and assumed
humility (Colossians 2.18, 23). In all other cases it describes the
Christian's essential attitude to his fellow-men. That which will
always give this word its meaning and its greatness is that
tapeinos, its corresponding adjective, is a self-description of
Jesus Christ. Jesus said: 'I am meek and lowly in heart'
(Matthew 11.29). *Tapeinophrosunē* describes the disposition in
which there is no self-assertion, no self-display, no self-seeking,
no wrong pride, no false ambition, nothing which would divide
a man from his fellow-men, and nothing which would give him
a false valuation of himself.

Tapeinophrosunē is the word in which the essential
difference of the Christian ethic is summarized. In Aristotle we
have the picture of the best of all characters, the man who is
megalopsuchos, 'great-souled' (Aristotle, *Nicomachean Ethics*,
IV. iii. 3-34). Let us look at that picture. The great-souled man
is the man who claims much and who deserves much. Any one
who claims less than he deserves is small-souled, especially
when his deserts are great. Now, the greatest claim of all is the
claim to honor, and it is that claim that the great-souled man
makes. Therefore, he must be a good man. When he is set in
honor, he feels that he is only receiving that which is due to him.
To all other things than honor he will be quite indifferent;
therefore, the great-souled man will give the impression of

being a haughty man. He will have a certain contempt of other people who are lesser souls; and, being such as he is, he is justified in despising others. He is fond of conferring benefits, but he is ashamed to receive any benefit. He desires always, not to be in any one's debt, but to put others in his debt. He will remember any benefit he has conferred, but will forget any benefit he has received, and will hate to be reminded of it. He will never ask for help, or only with the greatest reluctance. He will never go into any situation or society where any one else has the first place. He will be very outspoken, because he despises other men. He will be incapable of living at the will of any one else. He will lack the quality of admiration, for nothing seems great to him. He will bear no grudge and will never be interested in gossip, because he is entirely uninterested in other people. He likes things which are beautiful and useless rather than things which are useful.

Such, then, is Aristotle's picture of the great-souled man; and it is not far from being the antithesis of *tapeinophrosunē*. In the presence of God the Christian man will always have the humility of the creature before his Creator; and in the presence of his fellow-men the Christian man will always have the consciousness that he is amongst men as one who serves. 'Humility,' said Chrysostom, 'is the cause of all good. . . . Haughtiness is the first act of ingratitude, for it denies the gift of grace.'

Tapeinophrosunē involves the death of self, and makes it easy for a man to forget himself and to honor and to respect others.

(*b*) 'Look not on his own things'

Lastly, Paul insists that in Christian unity every man must 'look not on his own things,' but also on the things of others. The Greek verb which the A.V. translates 'to look' is *skopein*, and is stronger than that. It means in this case rather 'to concentrate upon.' So long as each man concentrates intensely upon himself and upon his own interests, there can be no such thing as unity; there can only be a competitive disintegration. It is when a man learns to concentrate as much upon others as upon himself that unity becomes a possibility. In other words, for Christian unity a man must learn to love his neighbor as himself.

So Paul sets before the Philippians the ideal of Christian unity. Christian unity implies a society where men think and act in harmony, a society in which each man lives in unconquerable benevolence to every other man, a society in which men share the very essential life principle which keeps them alive, a society in which there are no selfish ambitions, and no false self-valuations, a society where men live in the sense of their dependence on God, and of their debt and duty to others, a society in which men have learned to concentrate on the interests and the feelings of others as much as on their own.

We must now go on to see the appeal which Paul uses to move men's hearts to desire such a society, and the dynamic he offers to strengthen their wills to attain to it.

Paul's Fourfold Appeal

We have now seen how Paul sets before the Philippians the ideal of Christian unity; and we must go on to see how he urged and inspired them to overcome their dissensions and to rise to the height of that ideal.

He begins with personal appeal. Paul was not afraid to say to his converts: 'Do this for my sake!' It was perfectly natural that he should do so; his relation to his converts was not that of master to servant; it was not even that of teacher to pupil; it was that of father to child. Because there was love in his own heart, and because Paul knew that there was love in the heart of the Philippians, he does not hesitate to use the motive and the compulsion of love. Appeal was always nearer to Paul's mind than threat. In this appeal he uses a series of four phrases, all of which are in *v.* 1.

(*a*) 'Consolation in Christ'
'If there be any consolation in Christ', he says. The word for *consolation* is *paraklēsis*, which is never an easy word to translate. (i) It can mean exhortation to right living and to right action; it describes the pastor's urging of his people to be that which they ought to be, and that which in Christ they can be (Romans 12.8, I Corinthians 14.3, II Corinthians 8.17, I Thessalonians 2.3). (ii) It can mean comfort in sorrow and in distress, that which eases the pain of the heart (II Corinthians 7.13, Philemon 7). (iii) But the real flavor of the word is to be found in the company which it keeps. It appears in company with *oikodomē*, which means edification or upbuilding (I Corinthians 14.3); with *pathēmata*, which means sufferings (II Corinthians 1.7); with *thlipsis*, which describes the unceasing pressure of circumstances and events which are designed to hurt (II Corinthians 1.4, 7.4, 8.2); with *hupomonē*, which means 'a masculine constancy under trial', and which always has a background of courage and gallantry (Romans 15.4, 5). It is used in connection with the difficult mission of Titus to Corinth (II Corinthians 7.7); and it appears in connection with the command to stand fast (II Thessalonians 2.16). From this it is clear that *paraklēsis* most often has to do with that which gives a man the ability triumphantly to face a difficult, dangerous, or distressing situation. So Paul's first note of appeal is: 'Do you wish to give me strength and courage to face the hardships and the dangers of my imprisonment, that strength and courage which are to be found only in Christ? Then live at peace and in harmony with one another.'

(*b*) 'Comfort in Love'
'If there is any comfort in love', he says. The word for *comfort*

is *paramuthion*, an unusual word occurring only here in the New Testament. We shall see the flavor of this word from two classical usages of its corresponding verb *paramuthesthai*. In the *Phaedo* Plato describes the state of the soul when it is 'fastened and welded' to the body, and 'wallowing in utter ignorance'. This is caused by the lusts of the flesh, and the terrible characteristic of such a situation is that 'the prisoner is the chief assistant in his own imprisonment'. In such a situation 'philosophy, taking possession of the soul *encourages* it gently, and tries to set it free' (Plato, *Phaedo*, 83 A). Xenophon in his essay *On Hunting* describes how hounds should be treated when they are growing tired. The huntsman must encourage and *exhort* them gently frequently (Xenophon, *On Hunting*, vi. 25). The flavor of the word is a gentle and loving insistence on the right way and the right course of action. It is the pressure upon a man of some one who loves him to keep him on the right way, when there is much to make him abandon it in exhaustion and in despair. So Paul's second appeal is: 'Do you wish to give me love's encouragement in my present troubles? Do you wish to do something to assuage my anxiety and to enable me to go on? Then live at peace and in harmony with one another.'

(*c*) 'Fellowship of the Spirit'

'If there is any fellowship of the Spirit', he says. The words are *koinōnia pneumatos*. *Koinōnia*, of course, became the great word for Christian fellowship, but in ordinary Greek it can be used for a partnership of any kind. It can be used of partnership in a business, and a man's *koinōnos* is his business partner. In the Papyri father writes to his son complaining that their *koinōnos* in an allotment which they jointly own is not doing his share of the work. It can be used of the marriage partnership. In marriage two people have *koinōnia* of life, and on a tablet to his dead wife a Greek doctor says: 'I *shared* all life with you alone'.

The essence of the word is partnership. We think that in this case it gives better sense to take *pneumatos* as a subjective genitive, rather than as an objective genitive. The phrase does not mean *a share in the Holy Spirit*; it means *the partnership and fellowship, which only the Holy Spirit can give*. So Paul's third appeal is: 'Do you wish to enter into a real partnership with me? Do you wish to enter into that kind of partnership which only the Holy Spirit can initiate and cement? Then live at peace and in harmony with one another.'

(*d*) 'Bowels and mercies'

'If there are any bowels and mercies', he says. The words are *splanchna* and *oiktirmoi*. The word *bowels* appears strange to us in this context. But both to Greeks and to Jews what are known as the nobler viscera, that is, the heart, the lungs, the liver and the intestines, were held to be the seat of the emotions. So, then, the word means that kind of emotion which moves a man to the depths of his being. It describes no fleeting, superficial and sentimental feeling of emotion; it describes the emotion which penetrates into a man's inmost being.

But the real interest and impact of this phrase emerge when we investigate the biblical usage of the word *oiktirmos*. It occurs in four other New Testament passages, and in three of these passages the reference is to God. In Romans 12.1 Paul uses *the mercies of God* as a spur and stimulus to the Christian to devote his whole life to God. In II Corinthians 1.3 God is the God of *mercies*. In Colossians 3.12 those who are the elect of God must clothe themselves with *mercies*. This reference to God might be taken as only accidental, if we confine our investigation to the New Testament; but in the Septuagint out of twenty-six occasions on which this word occurs twenty-three are references to the mercy of God. The conclusion is inescapable. *Oiktirmos* is a word which characteristically refers to nothing other than the mercy of God. Paul is appealing to the Philippians to show to him that mercy and compassion which are a reflection of the mercy of God. So Paul's fourth appeal is: 'Do you really wish to show your heartfelt sympathy for me? Do you wish to show to me the mercy God shows to those who are in distress? Then live in peace and in harmony with one another.'

Here, then, in Paul's fourfold appeal to the Philippians. 'Do you really wish to give me the strength and courage, which can be found in Christ alone, to help me to meet my present situation? Do you really wish to give me love's encouragement in my present troubles? Do you really wish to demonstrate that ours is a perfect partnership, such as only the Holy Spirit can provide? Do you really wish to show to me a heartfelt sympathy which is like the mercy of God? Then live at peace and in harmony with one another.'

The Example of Christ

Although Paul does not hesitate to use the motive of personal appeal in his appeal for unity, he does not stop there. Unity in the Philippian Church may be desirable to ease Paul's anxiety and to bring him joy, but it is essential, if the example of Christ is to be followed and obeyed; Paul may begin by saying, 'For my sake', but he ends by saying, 'For Christ's sake'. So Paul moves on to the example of Christ. He introduces this final appeal with a difficult phrase in *v. 5*: *touto phroneite en humin ho kai en Christō Jēsou*. There is considerable discussion as to what this phrase means. The A.V. translates: 'Let this mind be in you, which was also in Christ Jesus'. The R.V. translates: 'Have this mind in you, which was also in Christ Jesus'. The R.S.V. translates: 'Have this mind among yourselves, which you have in Christ Jesus'. Moffat translates: 'Treat one another with the same spirit as you experience in Christ Jesus'. We have already seen that the verb *phronein* describes, not any single individual thought, but rather a man's whole attitude to life, the entire cast and atmosphere of his mind. The problem lies in deciding what verb is to be supplied in the relative clause *ho kai en Christō Jēsou phroneite*. The A.V. and the R.V. supply simply *is*; but it is clear that it is far more natural to supply *phroneite*, which is the verb of the main clause. It would also be much more natural to take the phrase *en Christō Jēsou* in the sense which is so typical and characteristic of Paul, as expressing the intimate and close and mystical relationship of the Christian to Christ, which can only be expressed by saying that the Christian is 'in Christ'. We suggest that what Paul is saying here in a highly compressed form may be expanded and paraphrased as follows: 'Have the same attitude to life always as you have when in your highest moments you are in Christ Jesus, and when you are fully one with him'. Paul is not making any new demand of the Philippians; he is not presenting them with a standard of conduct of which they have hitherto been ignorant; he is calling upon them to remember that which they already know, and that which in their highest moments they accept and practice.

So Paul goes on to place before the Philippians the example of Jesus Christ; and he does so by presenting a series of great contrasts between that which Jesus is eternally and by right, and that which by his own free choice he for a time became for the sake of men.

(*a*) 'In the form of God' – 'in fashion as a man'
Jesus Christ was *en morphē theou huparchōn*, 'in the form of God', but *schēmati heuretheis hōs anthrōpos*, was 'found in fashion as a man'. The verb *huparchein* is properly used in two ways. It describes what a person was in origin; and it is used of those qualities and characteristics which are the essential possession of a man, because they are part of himself. Paul, then, begins by saying that Jesus Christ was essentially and originally

in the form of God. This is underlined by the distinction between the two words *morphē* and *schēma*. The distinction between these two words is this – *morphē* is the unchanging form of a person or thing; *schēma* is the outward and the changing appearance. To take two examples – Africans, Indians, Chinese, Japanese, Europeans have different *schēmata*; but they have all the same *morphē*; they are all men. Externally they are different to look at, but beneath the changing exterior they are all men. Tulips, daffodils, roses, chrysanthemums, dahlias, delphiniums have different *schēmata*, but they all have the same *morphē*; they are all flowers. Plutarch uses both the verbs connected with these nouns in the seventh chapter of this essay *How to tell a Flatterer from a Friend*. The flatterer is like water; he changes his shape (*suschēmatizesthai*) to fit his receiver. He is like a changing chameleon, or a mirror which reflects what it sees. On the other hand, he speaks of the transformation (*metamorphousthai*) of the sailors into pigs in Circe's house. The flatterer changes only his outward form; the essential form of the sailors was changed.

The distinction between these two words is well seen in the New Testament itself. In Romans 12.2 Paul insists that the Christian must be transformed from the world (*metamorphousthai*); the Christian through Christ becomes a new creation. In II Corinthians 11.13-15 Paul speaks of those who transform themselves into apostles, and of Satan being transformed into an angel of light (*metaschēmatizesthai*). The false apostles and Satan change the externals but remain the same. So what Paul is saying here is that Jesus Christ is eternally and essentially in the form of God, and that for a time he took upon himself the outward form of a man. His godhead is utterly permanent; his manhood was temporary. This is exactly what the writer to the Hebrews meant when he spoke of Jesus being for a little while made lower than the angels (Hebrews 2.9 [R.V. margin, R.S.V., Moffatt]).

(*b*) 'The form of a servant'

But, if Paul had left the matter there, it is clear that such a way of speaking could have been used to further the tenets of Docetism and to belittle the reality of the Incarnation; to leave the matter there might seem to say that the Incarnation was simply an outward change with no inner reality. So Paul goes on to say of Jesus *morphēn doulou labōn*, He 'took upon himself the form of a servant'. The very use of the word *morphē* here lays down the reality of the Incarnation. Here was no play-acting, no change of outward form, no mere alteration of appearance. Just as Jesus really was God, so he really became a man and a servant.

(*c*) 'In the likeness of men'

Paul has still another phrase to add. He says of Jesus Christ *en homoiōmati anthrōpōn*, He 'was made in the likeness of men'. This phrase has two things to say of the Incarnation. First, the used of the word *genomenos* shows that the Incarnation was an episode in the life of Jesus Christ in contrast with the permanance of his glory and his godhead. *Gignesthai* always has the idea of *becoming*; it describes that which happens but which is not permanent. The Incarnation was a reality, but it was something which happened and ended, in contra-distinction to the endless godhead of Jesus Christ. Second, the phrase *en homoiōmati anthrōpōn* describes at one and the same time the identity of Jesus Christ with men and his difference from men. Dr Vincent Taylor in *The Person of Christ* makes two quotations which illustrate this. Luther said of Jesus: 'He ate, drank, slept, waked; was weary, sorrowful, rejoicing; he wept and he laughed; he knew hunger and thirst and sweat; he talked, he toiled, he prayed . . . so that there was no difference between *him* and other men, save only this, that he was *God* and had no sin'. Emil Brunner says: 'The Son of God in whom we are able to believe, must be such a One that it is possible to mistake him for an ordinary man'. In this passage it is precisely this truth that Paul lays down, the truth that Jesus Christ was a man in the fullest sense of the term, and that at the same time he was more than a man.

(*d*) 'Equal with God'
Paul then goes on to state another of these tremendous contrasts of which this passage is full. As the A.V. has it: 'Being in the form of God, [he] thought it not robbery to be equal with God, but made himself of no reputation'. The Greek text is: *ouch harpagmon hēgēsato to einai isa theō alla heauton ekenōsen*. The word which the A.V. translates *robbery* is *harpagmos*. The general rule is that nouns which end in *-mos* are active and describe a process. It is true that that is not an absolute rule; *thesmos* means an ordinance, that which is laid down; and *chrēsmos* means an oracle, a Divine answer which is given. But *harpagmos* is so rare a word that it is better to retain its most obvious meaning. If *harpagmos* be taken actively, Paul will be saying that Jesus Christ did not consider his own equality with God as an act of seizure and of plundering. There was no necessity that he should do so, for that equality was his and his by right. We must note that that which is Jesus Christ's by right is expressed in Greek by *to einai isa theō*, not by *to einai isos theō*. What is the difference? To use the phrase *isos theō* would mean that Jesus Christ possessed an absolute personal equality with God; to use the phrase *isa theō* means that the existence which Jesus Christ had in his glory was an existence which possessed and enjoyed all the privilege and the glory of God. Of that glory and these privileges he emptied himself (*heauton ekenosen*). Here Paul is saying what he had already said to the Corinthians: 'Though he was rich, yet for your sakes he became poor' (II Corinthians 8.9).

(*e*) The climax of humiliation

Finally in his description of the sacrifice of Jesus Christ Paul builds up a kind of climax of humiliation.

(i) 'He humbled himself' (*etapeinōsen heauton*). *Etapeinōsen* is an aorist tense, and, therefore, it describes one definite act in past time. This means that the humiliation which Jesus underwent was the outcome of a deliberate and spontaneous act of choice. As it has been said, one of the most moving sweeps of thought in this passage is that for Paul the sacrifice of Jesus began, not in time when he came to this earth, but in eternity.

(ii) 'He became obedient.' Surely it is indeed a Divine paradox to think of the King of kings and the Lord of lords becoming obedient. That he should *exact* obedience would be natural; that the should *render* obedience is the miracle of grace.

(iii) 'He became obedient unto death.' Here is the amazing fact that the Lord of life accepted death. As Charles Wesley put it in his hymn:

'Tis mystery all! The Immortal dies.

(iv) 'He became obedient unto death, even the death of the cross.' Even the ancient world regarded a cross with a kind of shuddering horror. Cicero writes: 'To bind a Roman citizen is an outrage; to scourge him a crime; it almost amounts to parricide to put him to death; how shall I describe crucifixion? No adequate word can be found to represent so execrable an enormity' (*In Verrem*, v. 66). 'Far be the very name of a cross', he says, 'not only from the body, but even from the thought, the eyes, the ears of Roman citizens' (*Pro Rabirio*, v. 10). The sacrifice of Christ was such that he accepted a death the horror of which was beyond words to tell.

Here, then, is the final appeal of Paul to the Philippians. If Jesus Christ was prepared to accept this amazing humiliation, how can his followers quarrel among themselves about matters of honor and of precedence? Surely all human thoughts of the exaltation of self must shrivel up before the memory of the amazing sacrificial selflessness of Jesus Christ.

Beyond the humiliation

But Paul does not end with the humiliation of Jesus Christ; he goes beyond the humiliation into the glory. Because of what he did, Jesus Christ is highly exalted and has been given the name which is above every name, so that the day will come when the whole universe will confess that Jesus Christ is Lord.

What is the name which Jesus Christ has received? There can be little doubt that the name which was in Paul's mind is *Kurios* which we translate *Lord*. It is one of the disasters of religious language that the title 'Lord' is so often glibly, conventionally and meaninglessly applied to Jesus. The word *kurios* has six stages in meaning, and, when we put them all together, we have a one word confession of faith. (i) It means *owner*, as when it is used for the owner of the vineyard (Matthew 20.8). (ii) It means *master*, as when it is used of the master in contradistinction to the slave (Matthew 25.18). (iii) It is the normal *title of respect* like Sir in English, as when it is used by the courteous, but disobedient, son (Matthew 21.30). (iv) It was the regular *title of the Roman Emperor*, who from the time of Domitian was *Kurios kai theos*. (v) The heathen regularly prefixed it to the names of their gods, as when a man spoke of 'My lord Serapis'. (vi) In the Septuagint it is the regular translation of Jahweh, the sacred name. To call Jesus Christ *Kurios* is to say that he is the master and the owner of our lives, the one to whom we give our respect, the one who is Divine, the one who is King and Emperor of life, the one who is nothing less than God. That is what a man *ought* to mean when he speaks of the Lord Jesus.

Two last points

Before we end our thinking about this passage, we may note two last things about it.

It must always be remembered that Paul's purpose in writing this passage was entirely practical. His aim was not to produce a theology or a Christology, but to bring into harmony those who were at variance with one another. And yet to do so he talked about the deepest things of the Christian faith. The early Protestant theologians insisted that 'doctrines must be preached practically and duties doctrinally'. And no passage shows better than this that a man's attitude to life, to himself, and to his fellow-men is a product of his attitude to Christ. It is a common demand that we should keep the Christian ethic and abandon the Christian theology, but here is the proof that ethics and theology must always walk hand in hand.

Last of all, we may note the extraordinary fascination this passage has had for Christian thinkers in all generations. In the old legend which tells how Thaddeus went to visit Abgarus, King of Edessa, there is an account of the preaching of Thaddeus: 'I will preach in their presence . . . concerning the coming of Jesus, how he was born; and concerning his mission, for what purpose he was sent by the Father; and concerning the power of his works, and the mysteries he proclaimed in the world, and by what power he did these things; and concerning his new preaching, and his abasement and humiliation and how he humbled himself and died and debased his divinity and was crucified' (Eusebius, *The Ecclesiastical History*, I. xiii. 19). A passage like that is instinct with memories of the words of Paul. R. C. Trench in his *Commentary on the Epistles to the Seven Churches* quotes a passage from Nicolaus Cabasilas, a fourteenth century Greek mystic: 'His love for men emptied God. He does not remain at a distance when he calls to himself the servant whom he loved, but he himself comes down and seeks him. To bring him back he who is rich came near to him who is poor. He came himself to tell his love and to seek an answering love. He does not abandon him who rejects him; he does not grow angry in face of insult; even when he is persecuted, he still waits at the doors. To show his love he does all things, and accepts his travail and dies'. There, again, are the echoes of Paul.

This is a passage whose meaning has left the most erudite theologian still seeking; but even the simplest person can find in it a rule for life, and an inspiration to devotion to, and to adoration of, Jesus Christ the Lord.

2
John 1.1-14:
Fully Man and Fully God

Chiefest of the Gospels

To very many the Fourth Gospel is the high-water mark of the
New Testament. 'Chiefest of the Gospels', Luther called it,
'unique, tender and true.' Very early in the history of
interpretation the four living creatures of the Revelation were
taken as symbols of the four Gospels (Revelation 4.7). The
allocation of the symbols varies; but in Augustine the symbol of
John was the eagle 'because John took a higher flight, and soared
in his preaching much more sublimely than the other three'
(*Homilies on John*, 36). The eagle is said to be the only living
creature which can look straight into the light of the sun, and not
be dazzled; so John, it was said, can look more directly into the
blazing light of truth than any other writer. It is of interest to note
that of all the New Testament writers John is the first definitely to
be said to be inspired (*pneumatophoros*) in the technical sense of
the term (Theophilus of Antioch, *Ad Autol.*, ii. 22).

If the Gospel itself reaches the highest level of New
Testament thought, many would say that the Prolog reaches
the highest level of thought within the Gospel. It might be held
that the identification of Jesus Christ with the Word, the Logos,
is one of the highest reaches of New Testament thought, and
that it is a conception which lends itself to reinterpretation in
every age and in every generation. In view of that it is strange
that Dr. Vincent Taylor in *The Person of Christ* (pp. 110,111)
expresses the view that the idea of the Logos is one which has

now little to say. He quotes E. F. Scott as saying that the idea of the Logos 'was an artificial hypothesis, and was utterly inadequate to set forth the true significance of the revelation in Jesus Christ'. He quotes Dr. Leonard Hodgson as saying that the association of the Logos idea with the doctrine of the Trinity has 'outlived its usefulness'. Dr. Taylor himself considers it a pertinent question to ask 'whether the subsequent course of Christological speculation might have been pursued more happily, without the excessive intellectualism which the Logos idea fostered'. In its day, as Dr. Taylor sees it, the Logos idea had its providential purpose, but 'it is not an idea with which Christian thought of today can set out with confidence on its Christological quest'.

It must be admitted that such verdicts come to us with a sense of shock; and they make it clear that there is a real need for a re-examination of the value of the Logos idea as an interpretation of the meaning of Jesus Christ.

Let us first of all look at the peculiar character of the Fourth Gospel. It is of very considerable interest that almost every account that we possess of the origin of the Fourth Gospel makes it the production of the Church rather than of an individual. In almost every account the impulse to write came rather from the Church than from the John who wrote it. Clement of Alexandria tells us that John was the last to write his Gospel, and that he 'noticing that the physical things had been set forth in the (other) Gospels, *being urged by his companions*, and inspired by the Spirit, wrote a spiritual Gospel' (quoted in Eusebius, *The Ecclesiastical History*, VI. xiv. 5). Jerome declares that John wrote his Gospel because *he was asked by the bishops of Asia* to do so to defend the faith against the heresies of Cerinthus (Jerome, *De Vir. Ill.*, ix). He was *urged by almost all the bishops of Asia at that time and by delegates of many Churches* to write more profoundly about the divinity of the

Savior (Jerome, *Commentary on Matthew*); and when he did
write the Prolog he was, in Jerome's phrase, *revelatione
saturatus*, saturated with revelation. Eusebius tells us that John
had passed all his time in proclaiming the gospel, and wrote
only under pressure, because he was asked to give an account of
the period in the ministry of Jesus which had been omitted by
the other writers (Eusebius, *The Ecclesiastical History*, III. xxiv.
6-11). The tenth-century *Codex Toletanus* prefaces the New
Testament books with short descriptions, and of the Fourth
Gospel it says: 'The apostle John, whom the Lord loved most,
last of all wrote this gospel, *at the request of the bishops of Asia*,
against Cerinthus and other heretics'. Finally, we may note the
account of the Muratorian Canon: '*When his fellow-disciples
and bishops urged John*, he said: "Fast together with me today
for three days and, what shall be revealed to each, let us tell it
to each other". On the same night it was revealed to Andrew,
one of the Apostles, that, with all of them reviewing it, John
should describe all things in his own name.' It is, of course,
impossible to accept that account as literally true; the presence
of Andrew could not have been possible; but once again the
communal character of the Gospel is clear.

The importance of the Fourth Gospel is vastly increased, if
we accept this fact which tradition so strongly and consistently
attests, that the writing of that Gospel was in some sense due to
the will of the Church. The tradition as it stands would lead us
to believe that the Gospel was written to defend the purity of
the Christian faith and the reality of the Incarnation against the
heretical thinking of Cerinthus and the like, and no doubt that
is in part true. But there was a much deeper reason why the
Fourth Gospel was written, and why it begins as it does.

The Double Background
Christianity was cradled in Judaism, but it was destined for the

world; but any truth must be stated in categories which those to whom it is preached can grasp and understand. Here was the problem. Christianity had hitherto been stated in Hebrew terms, and now it had to go out to the Greek world. E. J. Goodspeed (*An Introduction to the New Testament*, 297, 298) states the problem and the solution: 'To meet the needs of this Greek public some adjustments had to be made. Christianity was addressing it in Jewish terms. A Greek who felt like becoming a Christian was called upon to accept Jesus as the Christ, the Messiah. He would naturally ask what this meant and would have to be given a short course in Jewish apocalyptic thought. Was there no way in which he might be introduced directly to the values of the Christian salvation without being forever routed, we might even say detoured, through Judaism? Must Christianity always speak in a Jewish vocabulary? . . . Was there no way in which Christian truth could be stated in forms that would be immediately intelligible and welcome to the Greek mind? The times demanded that Christianity be transplanted to Greek soil and translated into universal terms. The Gospel of John is the response to this demand.' Here, then, is the *raison d'être* of the Fourth Gospel, and especially of its Prolog. The Fourth Gospel is the great – and successful – attempt to express something of the meaning of Jesus Christ in terms that *both* the Jew and the Greek could understand.

Jewish Thought
Let us, then, look at this double background of the conception of the Word, and let us begin with its Jewish background.

(*a*) The Word is alive
It is basic to remember that for the Jew a word was very much more than a mere sound. To the Jewish mind a word did things. A word was 'a concrete reality, a veritable cause' (G. F. Moore,

Judaism in the First Centuries of the Christian Era, i. 414). 'The spoken word to the Hebrew was fearfully alive. It was not simply a vocable or sound dropped heedlessly from unthinking lips. It was *a unit of energy charged with power*. It flies like a bullet to its billet. It is energized for weal or for woe' (John Paterson, *The Book that is Alive*, 2, 3). If that is true of any word, how much truer must it be of the word of God? The word of God is 'like a hammer that breaketh the rock in pieces' (Jeremiah 23.29). 'By the word of the Lord were the heavens made' (Psalm 33.6). God's word goes forth and does not return to him void, but accomplishes the purpose for which it was sent (Isaiah 55.11). For Hebrew thought there is dynamic energy in any word, and most of all in the word of God. In the Creation story each act of Creation is introduced by the phrase, 'And God said'. 'And God said, Let there be light: and there was light' (Genesis 1.3). We begin, then, with a conception which is deeply rooted in Hebrew thought, the conception of any word, and especially of the word of God, as an effective and creative power.

(*b*) To avoid irreverence – the Memra

By the middle of the third century B.C. Aramaic was displacing Hebrew as the language of the Jews. The Hebrew scriptures had to be translated into Aramaic, and these translations are the *Targums*. In the original Hebrew of the Old Testament on many occasions human feelings, actions and reactions are attributed to God; God is spoken of in terms and in terminology taken from human experience. Often the picture of God is anthropomorphic. By the time the *Targums* were emerging religious thought was becoming refined; these anthropomorphisms were regarded as belonging to the childhood of religion, and were felt to be an improper way of speaking of God. This was the age when men were beginning to be haunted by the idea of the sheer transcendence of God. In such cases the word *Memra*, which means *word*, is often substituted for God and the name of God. In the *Targums* *Memra* becomes a reverent circumlocution for God, when God, in the opinion of contemporary orthodoxy, was too anthropomorphically described. 'Moses brought forth the people out of the camp to meet with God' (Exodus 19.17) becomes, Moses brought forth the people before the *Memra*, the word, of God. It is no longer God, but the *Memra*, who is a consuming fire (Deuteronomy 9.3). Isaiah has the gloriously poetical picture: 'Mine hand also hath laid the foundation of the earth, and my right hand hath spanned the heavens' (Isaiah 48.13); but in the *Targum* this becomes, 'By my *Memra* I have founded the earth, and by my strength I have hung up the heavens'. Deuteronomy has the precious picture of the everlasting arms underneath and about us (Deuteronomy 33.27); but the *Targum* has it, 'The eternal God is thy refuge, and by his *Memra* the earth was created'.

In the *Targums* the expression *the word of God* becomes scattered here, there and everywhere throughout the Old Testament. We do not argue that the *meaning* of this phrase is anything like the meaning of Logos as John used it; but the fact remains that the continual usage of the phrase familiarized the ear with the expression *the word of God*.

(c) Wisdom
In the Wisdom Literature of the Jews the conception of Wisdom, *Sophia*, began to hold a very special place. Wisdom became, as it were, almost personalised. In particular Wisdom became a pre-existent power, who had been associated with God in the work of creation. In Proverbs Wisdom says: 'I was from everlasting, from the beginning, or ever the earth was . . . When he prepared the heavens I was there: when he set a compass on the face of the waters, when he established the

clouds above, when he strengthened the fountains of the deep, when he gave to the sea his decree that the waters should not pass his commandment, when he appointed the foundations of the earth, then was I by him, as one brought up with him, and I was daily his delight rejoicing always before him' (Proverbs 8.1-912). 'Wisdom hath been created before all things. . . . he created her . . . and poured her out on all his works' (Sirach 1.1-10). 'I came forth from the mouth of the Most High, and covered the earth as a mist' (Sirach 24.3-5). 'He created me from the beginning of the world, and to the end I shall not fail' (Sirach 24.9). In the Wisdom of Solomon it is Wisdom who fills the world and holds all things together (7.27). She was present at creation and was the instrument of God's creating work (9.1, 2, 9). She is the breath of the power of God, and the clear effluence of the glory of the Almighty (7.22ff.). Now clearly the function of this Wisdom is the same as the function of the creating Word of God; and the result was that the conception of the Word began to gain color and body and personality and vividness from the material which the descriptions of Wisdom supplied. The idea of the Word was becoming more and more meaningful and alive.

Greek Ideas
In his Hebrew heritage John had much with which to clothe the conception of the Word. But it is even more to the Greek background that we must turn. It was in Ephesus that John was writing about A.D. 100; it was with the Greeks that he was seeking a point of contact. It was with them in mind that he minted this conception of the Word. And the conception of the Word, the Logos, was deep in Greek thought.

(a) Heraclitus
It is strange, and maybe it is more than coincidence, that it was in Ephesus in the sixth century B.C. that we first hear of the

Logos. It was connected with the name of Heraclitus. Heraclitus had two basic ideas. He declared that everything is in a state of flux; nothing ever remains the same. It is quite impossible, he says, to step into the same river twice, for wave succeeds wave, and the river is always a different river. But in spite of that there is a certain continuity; in spite of that the world is not a chaos, but a cosmos. What is it that keeps it so? What gives the orderly, unchanging pattern amidst the eternal flow and flux? The answer is, the Logos. 'All things happen according to the Logos.' The Logos is the eternal principle of order in the universe; the Logos is that which is behind the flux, and that which makes the world a cosmos, an ordered whole.

(*b*) Stoicism

It was in Stoicism that the idea of the Logos came to its peak. The Stoic lived in a world which was God. God, said the Stoic, is fiery spirit and everything is God. At its purest the fiery spirit is God. A spark of it lodges in man and gives him life and reason. It becomes 'depotentiated' into matter; but even when it is depotentiated, it is still God; everything is God. Now the Stoic was fascinated by the order of the universe. What makes the seasons come and go in unvarying order? What makes the tides ebb and flow? What keeps the stars in their courses and solves the traffic problem of the heavens? What makes man a reasonable creature, and this universe an ordered and dependable whole? The answer was the Logos. And what was the Logos? The Logos was the mind of God, at one and the same time interpenetrated through all things, and guiding, controlling and directing all things. The Logos is the mind of God creating and sustaining the universe.

(*c*) Philo of Alexandria

There remain certain other strands to fit into this pattern; and by far the most important is Philo. Philo, born in 20 B.C. and still alive in A.D. 41, was an Alexandrian Jew. He was skilled in Jewish knowledge, and he was equally skilled in the wisdom of the Greeks. He was the bridge between the two worlds of thought. He was a voluminous writer, and in his works the Logos is referred to more than twelve hundred times. To him the Logos was 'the oldest and the most generic of things which have come into being'. The Logos was created, but it was incorruptible and eternal. God is the Father of the Logos; Wisdom is the mother; and the Cosmos is the garment. The Logos is the image of God, the second God, the Logos is between the begotten and the unbegotten. The Logos is the instrument of God in creation; it is the thought of God stamped upon the universe. The pilot of the universe, holding the Logos as a tiller, steers all things. It is through the Logos that the universe holds together; the Logos is the indissoluble bond of the universe. The human mind is stamped in conformity to the Logos. The Logos is the pattern of the human soul. The wise man chooses the Logos as his pilot. The Logos is the river which makes glad the city of God, which is the human soul. The Logos has the power of a father and a husband. It is a physician. It is the commander in whose ranks the soul must enrol. It is the defensive armor, the spear-bearer and the champion. The Logos is the High Priest of the soul.

For Philo, the Logos is the mind of God, the instrument of creation, the bond of order, the reason and the moral sense of man, the bridge between God and man.

(*d*) The Hermetic Literature

There remains still one other strand. There exists a body of literature called the Hermetic literature. It is supposed to be the work of Hermes Trismegistus. Its importance is that it is really religious mysticism, and represents the line of thought which afterwards found expression in the Mystery Religions. In it also

the Logos figures. Very briefly its picture is as follows. Every
word is the expression of a mind; and the divine Logos is the
expression of the mind, the *nous*, of God. The Logos is the
reasonable expression of the mind of God as contrasted with the
boē, the meaningless, unintelligible noise of chaos. The Logos is
the Voice of Light. In the work of creation the Logos separated
the lower from the higher elements. It is said that the Logos
invades the ocean of chaos, and brings it to order; then it rushes
upon and over it like a mighty wind; and then, its work
completed, it leaps back to heaven to God. Here again we have
the creating and ordering Word, who is the companion of God,
and the expression of the mind of God.

Here, then, is the background which was in the mind and the
memory of John. Here was what he seized on as a point of
contact by which to present Jesus Christ to the Greeks. W. F.
Howard wrote that the Logos was 'a term widely used in the
centuries immediately before and after the beginning of the
Christian era, and its meaning would have been understood at
once in any company of educated men in Athens or Alexandria
or Ephesus, at the end of the first century' (W. F. Howard,
Christianity according to St. John, 34). William Manson writes
of the Prolog of the Fourth Gospel: 'The Jesus of Nazareth and
Galilee and the trial-hall and Calvary is here proclaimed to the
world as the Logos of God, as God's Self-utterance to men, as
God's Language and living Thought, as God's Eloquence, as
God's truth in action, as the measure of God's Mind, nay, as
One who, in His human life and suffering, is yet to be hailed as

> God's presence and His very self
> And essence all Divine'
>
> *(The Way of the Cross, 30)*

Jesus as the Logos
Let us then, before we go on to examine the Prolog in detail, ask

what is the broad truth that John is seeking to tell to men in his presentation of Jesus as the Logos?

It must always be remembered that the word Logos has two meanings; it means *mind* or *reason*; and it means *word*. That is why it is untranslatable, and that is why, for instance, Moffat does not try to translate it, but keeps the word Logos in his translation. Let us come at this, then, from both directions.

1. Logos means *reason*. John says to the Greeks: 'For centuries you have been talking about the Logos. You have been talking about that mind and reason of God which makes this world an ordered cosmos, that Logos which created the world, that Logos which sustains the world, that mind of God which is the creator and the sustainer of the universe. Well, then, *if you wish to see what that mind of God is like, look at Jesus Christ.* In this man Jesus the mind of God took flesh and became a person.'

2. Logos means a *word*. Here is the simpler approach, but the end is the same. What is the simplest definition of a word? The simplest definition of a word is that a word is the expression of a thought. So, then, John is saying: 'If you wish to see what God is thinking, if you wish to see how God thinks, *if you wish to see the expression of the thought of God, look at Jesus Christ.* In this man Jesus the thought of God took flesh and became a person.'

That is exactly what a Greek would understand when he heard that the Logos had become flesh. And when we do look at Jesus Christ what do we see? We see One who fed the hungry, healed the sick, comforted the sad, and was the Friend of outcast men and women. That, says John, is the mind of God. That is the expression of the thought of God. That is God's attitude to men.

Here was a revolution in the idea of God to the Greek world. The Stoic thought of God in terms of *apatheia*, which means *incapability to feel*. The Stoic argued that God, by definition, must be unable to feel anything. If God can feel joy or grief, it means that some one can make God glad or sad. That means that, for the moment, some one can influence God. That means that, for the moment, that person is greater than God, and can affect God. Therefore, in order that God may be Lord, and that that may never happen, God is essentially without any feeling at all. The Epicurean thought of God in terms of *detachment*. That there are gods, he allowed. But he insisted that these gods in their undisturbed serenity were utterly detached from the world. As Tennyson had it:

> For they lie beside their nectar, and the bolts are hurl'd
> Far below them in the valleys, and the clouds are lightly curl'd
> Round their golden houses, girdled with the gleaming world:
> Where they smile in secret, looking over wasted lands,
> Blight and famine, plague and earthquake, roaring deeps and
>   fiery sands,
> Clanging fights, and flaming towns, and sinking ships, and
>   praying hands.

John spoke to a world which thought of the gods in terms of passionless *apatheia* and serene *detachment*. He pointed at Jesus Christ and said: 'Here is the mind of God; here is the expression of the thought of God; here is the Logos'. And men were confronted with a God who cared so passionately and who loved so sacrificially that his expression was Jesus Christ and his emblem a cross.

Five Great Facts about Jesus
In the Prolog to his Gospel John deals with five great facts about Jesus Christ.

(*a*) What Jesus Is
He begins by stating *what Jesus Christ personally is*. 'The Word',

he says, 'was God' (*v.* 1). Moffat translates this, 'the Logos was divine'. The difficulty here is that neither the A.V. translation nor the Moffat translation is completely accurate. The Greek phrase is *theos ēn ho logos*. If there had been a definite article with *theos*, then the translation, 'the Word was God', would have been completely correct, for then the Word would have been completely identified with God; but, since there is no definite article, that which John is saying is very difficult to express in English. He is saying, to put it colloquially, that the Word is in the same class as God; or, to put it more technically, that the Word belongs to the same sphere of being as God. To say that the Word was God is too much; to say that the Word was Divine is too little. In this phrase John is saying what the whole New Testament is saying; he is saying that Jesus is a man, but that human categories are quite inadequate to contain him, and human classifications are quite inadequate to describe him. 'I know men', said Napoleon, 'and Jesus Christ was more than a man.' John is saying that, although Jesus of Nazareth was a human person, he nevertheless cannot be described in any other terms than in terms of God. And it must always be remembered that that is not so much a theological statement, worked out by the activity of the mind, as it is an affirmation of Christian experience, when a man is confronted with Jesus Christ.

John has already said that the Word was in the beginning and that the Word was with God. Here we are face to face with one of the most difficult of all ideas, the idea of the pre-existence of Christ. When we are thinking of this idea of pre-existence, it is of the greatest importance to remember that it was not an idea which John discovered or introduced; it was an idea which he found ready to hand. As we have already seen, Wisdom was with God in the beginning of His ways, before ever the earth was, before the mountains and the hills were brought forth, and when God prepared the heavens (Proverbs 8.22-30). In the

Book of Enoch that Son of Man, the Divine Messiah, was with God 'before the sun and the signs were created, before the stars of heaven were made' (48.3). God chose him and hid him before the creation of the world (48.6). From the beginning the Son of Man was hidden, 'and the Most High preserved him in the presence of his might' (62.7). The Messiah is he whom the Most High is keeping for many ages (4 Ezra 13.25-26). In the Rabbinic thought 'the advent of the Messiah is only an episode in the life of one who has existed from all time; King Messiah, it is said, pre-existed before the creation of the world' (W. O. E. Oesterley, *The Doctrine of the Last Things*, 131). In the *Shepherd of Hermas* it is taught that the Church pre-existed from all time. 'She was created first of all things. For this reason she is old; and for her sake was the world established' (*Visions*, II. iv. 1). What is even more significant is that in the instructions for the making of the furniture of the Tabernacle it is repeatedly indicated that these furnishings and their pattern already pre-existed in heaven with God (Exodus 25.9, 40, 26.30, 27.8, Numbers 8.4).

It is, then, clear that the idea of pre-existence is an idea that was familiar to Jewish thought. But what was meant by it? It seems most likely that the Jew meant something quite simple, when he talked of pre-existence; he meant that every good thing existed in the plan and the purpose and the mind of God, before it emerged into this world, and to the realm of space and time. Let us take this idea and let us apply it to the pre-existence of the Word, of Jesus Christ. We have seen that by calling Jesus the Word John means us to see in him the expression of the mind and of the thought of God. If that be so, it means that to say that Jesus pre-existed is to say that *God was and is always like Jesus Christ*. It means that there was no change in the attitude of God to men. There are certain theologies which seem to teach, or at least to imply, that Jesus Christ did something to alter the attitude of God to men; that somehow that work of Jesus Christ changed a God of wrath into a God of love; that before the work of Jesus Christ God was the stern and inexorable judge, and that after the work of Jesus Christ God was the loving and forgiving father. Nothing could be further from New Testament teaching. Whatever else the pre-existence of the Word means, it certainly does mean that God has always been, and still is, the God whose attitude to men is expressed in the life of sacrificial love which is the life of Jesus Christ. It may well be that this is not the whole truth in the idea of pre-existence, but it certainly is a truth even a simple mind can grasp and in which such a mind can rest.

(b) What Jesus Did

John goes on to state *what Jesus Christ did*. He goes on to insist on the part of the Word in creation, and to say that all things came into being through him, and that apart from him nothing was made (*v.* 3). This is an idea which was also an essential part of Pauline thinking. 'For by him were all things created, that are in heaven, and that are in earth, visible and invisible' (Colossians 1.16). The same idea is part of the thought of the writer to the Hebrews, who speaks of the Son by whom also God made the worlds (Hebrews 1.2). It will be seen that this is an idea which becomes explicit comparatively late in New Testament thought. It is true that as early as I Corinthians Paul can speak of the Lord Jesus Christ, by whom are all things (I Corinthians 8.6), but it is not until the end of his life that he brings this idea into the foreground of his thinking. This is a clear instance of the development of doctrine under the demand of circumstances. What, then, was the moving cause of this development, and what brought the creative work of the Son to the forefront of Christian belief?

In the Graeco-Roman world there was a tendency of thought which is summed up in the general term of Gnosticism. The main tenet of Gnosticism was that matter is evil and only spirit is good. Gnosticism further believed that matter is eternal. That is to say, this world is created out of material which is essentially flawed. God is spirit, and, if matter is essentially evil, it means that God himself could have no contact with matter; therefore, God himself is necessarily not the creator of the world. How, then, was the world created? From himself God put forth a series of aeons or emanations. Each of these emanations was further and further away from God. And each of these emanations was more and more ignorant of God, until there came a stage when ignorance of God became hostility and enmity to God. At the end of this series of aeons there at last came an aeon, which was so distant from God that it could touch and handle and mould and form this evil matter. That aeon was the creator of the world. Such is a very simplified account of the Gnostic idea of creation. It has the most far-reaching consequences, for it means that this world was created by a God who is ignorant of, and hostile to, the true God. The Gnostic commonly went on to hold that the ignorant and hostile creating God is the God of the Old Testament, while the true God is the God of the New Testament, and the God of Jesus Christ. It was in answer to this teaching of Gnosticism that Christian thought developed the idea of the Son as the creative agent of God. The Gnostic held that creation was evil; the Christian holds, as the old Genesis story so often repeats, that creation is good (Genesis 1.10, 12, 18, 21, 25). The Christian holds that this is God's world, and that the instrument and agent and moving cause of creation is God's Word.

What, then, is the practical consequence of this Christian conception for faith? To say that God's Word was God's agent and instrument in creation is to say that the principle on which the world is created is the same principle as we see in Jesus Christ. Creation also is an expression of the mind of God, and it is an expression of that same attitude of mind as we see in Jesus Christ. Lessing said that, if he had one question to ask the Sphinx, his one question would be: 'Is this a friendly universe?' Dick Sheppard told of an experience when he was one night alone in the dark, and when he felt the spirit of the universe all around him, and when he felt moved to cry out the question: 'Friend or foe?' The Christian doctrine of creation means that this is essentially a friendly universe, because creation is an expression of that same mind of God which is displayed in Jesus Christ. The world in which we live is meant, not to break us, but to make us. It is true that the sin of man has sometimes made ugly the beauty given by God; and the folly of man has sometimes turned the gifts of God in creation into the instruments of man's own ruin. But the fact remains that the Christian doctrine of creation means that the world is purposed and designed for the making of men and not for the destruction of man.

(c) What Jesus Became

John goes on to state *what Jesus became*. 'The Word', he says, 'was made flesh' (*v.* 14). For the Hellenistic world this was easily the most startling statement in the whole Gospel. Before Augustine became a Christian he was skilled in pagan thought and philosophy, and in the *Confessions* (vi. 9) he tells us that somewhere or other in the pagan thinkers he had read in one form or another nearly all the things which Christianity said, but one thing he had never read – 'The Word became flesh'.

The Gnosticism of which we have spoken was in reality only the development of a deeply rooted Greek tendency of thought. It is customary to speak of the Greeks as the most sunny-hearted of all peoples, but bit by bit the Greeks came to develop an acute sense of sin; and, arguing from experience, they regarded the body as the seat of sin. So as far back as the sixth century B.C.

the Orphics laid down the principle *sōma sēma*, the body is a tomb. 'The body is that which obstructs and fetters and which must be cast off.' Philolaus said that the body is a house of detention in which the soul is imprisoned to expiate its sin (*Frag.*, 14). Empedocles, who believed in the transmigration of souls, thought of the soul's weary pilgrimage through the bodies of men and animals and plants until at last it expiated its sin, and found release. This, too, is the doctrine of Plato. The study of philosophy is nothing other than the study of dying and of being dead. The soul can only reach out to reality when it avoids all association and contact with the body; the philosopher must necessarily despise the body. So long as we have a body, the soul is contaminated by evil and cannot attain the truth. Pure knowledge is impossible so long as the body is with us. The soul must strive to be freed from the body as from the fetters of a prison-house; and, therefore, death is alone desirable as the release (*Phaedo*, 64-67). The body is a tomb, and the soul is buried in this present life, shut up in an enclosure like a prison, undergoing punishment (*Cratylus*, 400 B.C.). There are few people who have hated the body as Epictetus did. The body is the filthiest and the most unpleasant of things; he is ashamed that he has a body; he likens himself to a poor soul shackled to a corpse (*Frag.*, 23). 'Disdain the flesh', urges Marcus Aurelius, 'blood and bones and network, a twisted skein of nerves, veins, arteries' (*The Meditations*, ii. 2). Seneca, in whom Stoicism came at its best to Rome, speaks of 'the detestable habitation of the body', and of the *inutilis caro*, the vain flesh, in which the soul is imprisoned while it pines for its celestial home (*Letters*, 92, 110). With one voice the ancient world united to damn the body as that which was the prison-house and tomb of the immortal soul.

That attitude of mind invaded the Church, and it was the concern of John to combat it. 'The Word', he insists, 'became flesh.' In the First Epistle the very test of Christianity is the confession that Jesus Christ did come in the flesh, and the denial of it is the spirit of antichrist (I John 4.2, 3). The heresy which denied the flesh and blood reality of the Incarnation was called Docetism, or, as Goodspeed suggests it might be translated, *Seemism*. It held that Jesus only *seemed* to have a body, that he was an unsubstantial phantom who never had a flesh and blood physical body. In the heretical *Acts of John* (93) John is depicted as saying of Jesus: 'Sometimes when I would lay hold of him, I met with a material and solid body, and at other times, again, when I felt him, the substance was immaterial, and as if it did not exist at all'. When Jesus walked, it is said in the same passage, he left no footprints on the ground at all. Cerinthus gave this heresy another twist. To anyone who held the tenets of Gnosticism it was utterly incredible that the Divine Being should experience suffering. So Cerinthus taught that the Christ came into the man Jesus at the Baptism, and left him before the Crucifixion. The *Acts of John* actually purport to give an account of a conversation between Jesus and John on the hillside at the very time when the Crucifixion was going on. The Christ is depicted as saying: 'John, unto the multitude down below in Jerusalem I am being crucified, and pierced with lances and with reeds, and gall and vinegar are given me to drink. But I am speaking to you, and listen to what I say. . . . Nothing, therefore, of the things they will say of me have I suffered.' How common and how threatening this view became may be seen from the *Letters* of Ignatius, who repeatedly insists that Jesus was truly born, truly ate and drank, was truly persecuted, was truly crucified, and truly died (Ignatius, *To the Trallians*, 9 and 10; *To the Smyrnaeans*, 2; cf. Polycarp, *To the Philippians*, vii. 1).

In a very real sense this is the most dangerous of all heresies, because it comes from a mistaken reverence; it comes from a shrinking from fully involving God in the world and in human life; it comes from seeking to be more spiritual than God. In his book *Inherit the Promise* (pp. 177-206) Dr. Pierson Parker has some very relevant things to say about this ever-recurring Gnostic heresy. It forgets the opening confession of the Nicene Creed: 'I believe in one God, the Father Almighty, Maker of *heaven and earth*, and of all things *visible and invisible*'. William Temple said: 'Christianity is the most avowedly materialist of all the great religions'. Christianity is the only religion which gives full weight to body and to spirit, to the seen and to the unseen world. The moment the balance is disturbed, and the moment either body or spirit usurps more than its proper place, the whole of life goes wrong. If the *body* is stressed solely, and all spiritual values are denied, then we get dialectical materialism, whose most familiar manifestation is Communism, or we get a humanistic social culture whose yardsticks are materialistic standards. If the *spirit* is solely stressed we get religions like Buddhism and Hinduism with their doctrines of *maya*, which teaches that all physical things and occurrences are evil, illusory, and to be despised.

In the very phrase, 'The Word became flesh', there lies the guarantee that flesh and spirit are both dear to God; there lies the inspiration of human life which comes from the fact that God did not hesitate to enter into that life; there lies the Christian challenge which insists that the world cannot be disregarded, and the world cannot be worshipped, but that the world must be redeemed. That it is possible to say, 'The Word became flesh', means that *soul* salvation must also be *whole* salvation.

(*d*) What Jesus Gives

John goes on to state *what Jesus Christ gives*. In the Prolog John presents Jesus as the giver of three gifts.

(1) He is the giver of *life*. It may literally be said that life is the beginning, the middle and the end of the Fourth Gospel. John begins by saying, 'In him was life' (1.4); he ends by saying that the Gospel was written to enable men to believe in Jesus Christ, and to have life through his name (20.31); and it is the central claim of Jesus that he came that men might have life, and that they might have it more abundantly (10.10). It may fitly be said that Jesus came to change existence into life. The Romans told how once a wretched man came to Julius Caesar asking for permission to commit suicide. Caesar looked at him. 'Man', he said, 'were you ever alive?' Jesus came to lift men out of a weary, drooping, defeated existence into a full, virile, victorious life. Browning draws a picture of the first glimpse which two lovers caught of each other. She looked at him, he says; and he looked at her; 'and suddenly life awoke'. In Jesus Christ the mere task of living becomes the real glory of life.

(2) He is the giver of *light*. The life is the light (*v.* 4). The only function of John the Baptist is to point men to the light which is Jesus Christ (*vv.* 6-8). He is the true light (*v.* 9). Here John uses one of his favorite words. The word which is translated *true* is *alēthinos*. John uses that word more than once in connection with Jesus. Jesus is the *true* bread (6.32); He is the *true* vine (15.1). There are in Greek two closely interrelated words, which are both translated *true*. There is *alēthēs*, which means *true* as a statement is true, and as a promise is true; it describes that which is true as opposed to that which is a lie. And there is *alēthinos*, which means *true* in the sense of *genuine*, *real*, as opposed to that which is unreal, without substance, that which is a substitute, that which is, in the war-time phrase, *ersatz*. Jesus, then, is the genuine light, the real light. Other lights may flash and fade; other lights may mislead and misdirect. He is the true light. A light has two great functions. A light *reveals*, and a light *guides*. Jesus reveals to men that

which their life is, and that which their life ought to be; and then, lest that terrible comparison between the actual and the ideal should drive them to despair, he leads them to the source of new life in himself.

(3) This leads us naturally to the third gift of Jesus Christ. He is the giver of the *new birth*. By the divine rebirth he gives men power to become the sons of God. When the Christian candidate emerged from baptism, he was clothed in new white robes to symbolize the fact that he had entered on a new life. The very word *candidatus* means *one who is clothed in white*. The difference which Jesus Christ makes to a man is so complete and so radical that nothing less is adequate to describe it than to call it a new birth. In him the coward becomes the hero, the sinner becomes the saint, and the man of the world becomes the man of God.

(*e*) What Jesus Suffered

Finally, the Prolog does not forget *what Christ suffered*. He was in the world which he had made, and the world did not recognize him; he came unto his own, and his own received him not (*vv.* 10-11). Here is the tragedy of the offered and rejected glory.

There are few passages in the New Testament which in so short a compass as these fourteen verses so set out the splendor of the glory of Christ, the greatness of the sacrifice of the Incarnation, the magnificent generosity of the offer of Christ, and the poignant tragedy of the rejection of Christ. In the Prolog John set out to present the gospel to the Greeks of Ephesus, but in so doing he left a picture which men will never be able to read in any age without an answering thrill within their hearts.

3
Romans 5.12-21:
Sin and Salvation

The Character and Purpose of Romans

The Letter to the Romans must always be central in any attempt to discover and to interpret the essence of the mind and thought of Paul. Romans is the nearest approach to a theological treatise that Paul ever wrote. For the most part Paul's letters were called forth by the immediate problems and perils which threatened his churches, and were produced to meet an immediate situation; but Dibelius says of Romans that of all Paul's letters it is least conditioned by the momentary situation.

Two great adjectives have been used to describe Romans. Sanday and Headlam called it *testamentary*. It is the testament of Paul; it is as if in it Paul sat down to distil the essence of his gospel and his faith in order to send an account of his essential belief to the Christian Church in the city which was the capital of the world. Burton called it *prophylactic*. Paul had never been in Rome when he wrote Romans, and had had no direct contact with the Church in Rome. But in all his churches he had seen the damage which could follow mistaken beliefs, misguided conceptions, ethical and theological eccentricities, false teaching and interrupted personal relationships. He, therefore, sent this letter to Rome so that, if any of these things did invade the Church at Rome, the Christians there might have a strong antiseptic and prophylactic to guard them against the poison and the infection of error.

Two interesting theories of the origin of Romans have been

advanced. It has been suggested that the material in the early part of Romans was originally the material which Paul prepared for presentation at the Council of Jerusalem, when the Gentiles were accepted into the membership of the Church. And, indeed, nothing could so clearly demonstrate the right of entry of the Gentiles into the Church as the demonstration that Justification by Faith is the central fact of the Christian life and experience.

But the second theory of the origin of Romans is even more likely to be correct. All his life Paul had been haunted by the desire to see Rome. When he was in Ephesus, he was planning to go through Achaia and Macedonia again; then comes the sentence, straight from the heart: 'After I have been there, I must also see Rome' (Acts 19.21). When things in Jerusalem were grim and threatening, he had a vision of the Risen Christ. The Lord stood by him and said: 'Be of good cheer, Paul: for as thou hast testified of me in Jerusalem, so must thou bear witness also at Rome' (Acts 23.11). In the letter itself he writes: 'I long to see you' (1.11); and again: 'So, as much as in me is, I am ready to preach the gospel to you that are at Rome also' (1.15). It was in Corinth in the year A.D. 58 that Paul wrote Romans, and Rome was very much in his mind and in his plans.

At the moment he was just about to bring to its completion a scheme which had been very dear to his heart. He was about to take to Jerusalem the collection for the poor of the Church of Jerusalem which he had raised from his other churches (Romans 15.25, 26). He knew that the journey to Jerusalem was fraught with danger, and that his enemies among the Jews would do their best to eliminate him, and he asks for the prayers of the Christians at Rome (Romans 15.30, 31). But there are still greater plans simmering in his mind. He is planning to go on to Spain. It so happened that at this time there was a kind of blaze of greatness in Spain. Martial, the master of the epigram, and Lucan, the epic poet, were Spaniards, as were Columella and

Pomponius Mela. Quintilian, the greatest of all the orators, was a Spaniard, and so was Seneca, dramatist, philosopher and prime minister of Nero. It would be something to touch for Christ a land which was producing such greatness. So Paul proposed to visit Rome on the Way to Spain (Romans 15.24, 28).

It is here that we may well have at one and the same time the reason why Paul wrote Romans and the reason for its centrality as an exposition of his thought and belief. When any general plans a new campaign, he must have a base of operations from which his lines may go out; and it may well be that Paul hoped to make Rome the basis of the campaign in the West, which he was planning. The people of Rome did not know Paul personally; he had neither founded the Church in Rome, nor had he ever visited it. So Paul may well have written this letter to enable the Roman Church to see exactly where he stood, and what he believed, and what he preached. Beyond a doubt mixed reports of him would have reached Rome, for Paul had his bitter enemies as well as his staunch friends; and Romans may well have been the declaration of his faith, so that, when the time came, the Roman Church might be ready and willing to receive him, when he set out on his campaign in Spain. Whether Paul ever reached Spain or not must remain uncertain, although the balance of probability is all against it; but, had his plans materialized, he certainly would have preached in Spain, and Rome would have been his base of operations.

There are indications that in the Early Church the Letter to the Romans did actually circulate as a compendium and manifesto of Pauline faith and belief. In our version of Romans the letter ends with a great doxology (16.25, 26). The textual history of that doxology is complicated and interesting and suggestive. We quote only the evidence of the uncial manuscripts in the following summary of it. The doxology appears at the end of the sixteenth chapter in A, B, C, D, E. It appears at the end of ch. 14 in L. It appears in both places in A and P. In the Chester Beatty papyrus it appears at the end of ch. 15. In G it appears in neither place, although a space is left for it. In certain Latin manuscripts, for example Amiatinus and Fuldensis, there is a system whereby the text is divided into sections, and a summary of each section supplied. In such manuscripts the last two summaries are as follows. '50. On the peril of him who grieves his brother by meat' (which must be a summary of 14.15-23). '51. On the mystery of the Lord kept secret before his passion, but after his passion revealed', which can only be the doxology. This must mean that these sections and summaries were made from a version of Romans which did not include chs. 15 and 16. That such a version existed we could already have deduced, for a doxology can only come at the end, and there are manuscripts, as we have seen, which have the doxology at the end of ch. 14. To all this we must add the final textual fact. G, the manuscript which omits the doxology in both places, also omits all mention of Rome in 1.7 and 1.15. According to it, the letter is written simply to all the beloved of God.

The conclusion of all this seems clear. Romans existed in two forms. It existed in the form in which we possess it; and it existed in a form from which all the local references had been removed, and from which the last two chapters had been taken away. That must most likely mean that the Early Church was so convinced that Romans had in it the very essence of Pauline faith and doctrine that at some time a version of Romans was produced from which all local references were removed, and in which the letter was used as a compendium of Pauline doctrine for the whole Church at large.

When we are seeking to interpret Romans, we do well to remember that we are dealing with a letter which the Church has always believed to have in it the very essence and distillation of Paulinism.

The Basic Problem of Life

The basic problem with which Romans deals is the basic problem of all life. It is the problem of how a man may enter into a right relationship with God. Paul looks at the pagan world; and it is clear that the pagan world with its blatant immorality and its moral frustration has not solved that problem (1.18-32). No one was more conscious of that failure than were the pagan writers themselves. Men, said Seneca, are overwhelmingly conscious of their weakness and their inefficiency in necessary things. Men, he says with a kind of pessimistic hopelessness, love their vices and hate them at the same time. They hate their sins and cannot leave them. As Ovid had put it in the famous lines:

> *Video meliora, proboque;*
> *Deteriora sequor.*

'I see and approve the better things, but I follow the worse' (*Metamorphoses*, vii, 20). It was pitilessly clear that the pagan world had not found the way to enter into a right relationship with God. Nor had the Jewish world. In this Paul spoke from experience. As touching the righteousness which was in the law he could claim to be blameless (Philippians 3.6), and yet, until Jesus Christ laid hands on him, he was conscious of nothing but moral helplessness, and spiritual estrangement from God. The reason for this failure is sin; and in our passage Paul deals with the origin of sin, with man's inescapable involvement in sin as a human being, and with God's method of dealing with the situation.

Jewish Thought about Sin

First, then, Paul deals with the origin of sin. It is Paul's argument that by one man, that is, by Adam, sin entered into the world. Before we begin to examine what Paul meant by that, and the inferences he drew from that, let us see from where Paul started. That is to say, let us see what Jewish thought between the Testaments had to say about the origin of sin.

(*a*) The universality of sin

Jewish thought recognized the universality of sin. 'All the earth-born are defiled with iniquities, full of sins, laden with offences' (4 Ezra 7.68). There is an 'innate evil thought in man' (4 Ezra 7.92). It was due to sin that death entered into the world. 'God created man for incorruption . . . but by the envy of the devil death entered into the world' (Wisdom 2.23, 24). But whence came that sin?

(*b*) 'By the envy of Satan'

To that question more than one answer was given. Sometimes it was held that the origin of sin was, so to speak, external to man. We have just seen that Wisdom says that it entered in 'by the envy of Satan'. In Enoch we read of an angel called Gadreel who 'showed the children of men all the blows of death, and led Eve astray (Enoch 69.6). In the Books of Adam and Eve (The Apocalypse of Moses, 19) the story is told of how in the Garden the Devil tempted Eve and made her promise to give the forbidden fruit to Adam. 'He went and poured upon the fruit the poison of his wickedness, which is lust, the root and beginning of every sin, and he bent the branch on earth and I took of the fruit and ate.' But this was no real solution; it only pushes the origin of sin one step further back, and it does not explain what it was within man which caused man to fall to temptation.

(*c*) The two natures

The commonest Jewish explanation of sin was found in what is really a recognition of human experience. It was found in the doctrine of the two natures – the *Yēṣer ha-ṭōb* and the *Yēṣer ha-ra'*, the good nature and the evil nature. It is a fact of universal human experience that in man there are two tendencies, one tendency which draws a man to goodness, and another tendency which draws a man to evil; and Jewish thought made much of the evil tendency in man. 'O evil tendency', laments Ben Sirach, 'wherefore wast thou created?' (Sirach 37.3). The Rabbis called the evil tendency 'the strange god within man' (Shabbath 105 b). They called it 'the spoiler who spares none, bringing men to fall even at the advanced age of seventy or eighty'. So powerful is this evil tendency, this *yēṣer ha-ra'*, that it can *become* the man. There is a rabbinic interpretation (Sukkah 52 b) of Nathan's parable to David (II Samuel 12.4). That verse reads: 'And there came *a traveler* unto the rich man, and he spared to take of his own flock and his own herd, to dress for *the wayfaring man* that was come unto him; but took the poor man's lamb, and dressed it for *the man* that was come to him'. That is said to be symbolic of the *yēṣer ha-ra'*. It comes to us first as *a traveler*; then it becomes *a guest*; and finally it becomes *a man* himself (quoted by Charles Taylor, *Sayings of the Jewish Fathers*, 149).

Having, then, installed the evil tendency in man as the origin and cause of sin, Jewish thought went in two directions. The first line of thought refused to absolve man for personal responsibility for his sin. The evil tendency was placed in man to be overcome, and God gave men the Law in order to counteract it, and constant study of the Law will enable a man to overcome it. Man is not in the unbreakable grip of an external power; he can and must choose. 'Sin has not been sent upon the earth, but man of himself has created it, and under a great curse shall they fall who commit it' (Enoch 98.4).

But the very strenuousness with which many of the Jewish writers insist on personal responsibility shows that there was another line of thought. The idea of the *yēṣer ha-ra'* has only pushed the question still one further step back. Whence came the *yēṣer ha-ra'*? It is here that Jewish rabbinic thought produced one of the most dangerous of all doctrines. God, they said, created all things, and, therefore, God created the *yēṣer ha-ra'*. True God also created the Law as a means of healing, but God created the evil tendency. 'God said, it repents me that I created the evil tendency in man; for if I had not done so, he would not have rebelled against me. I created the evil tendency; I created the Law as a means of healing. If you occupy yourself with the Law, you will not fall into the power of it. God placed the good tendency on a man's right hand and the evil on his left' (cf. the Midrash *Bereshith Rabba*, xxvii.; the Babylonian *Talmud*, *Qiddushin* 30 b).

Philo tries to avoid this conclusion. He takes the phrase, 'Let us make man' (Genesis 1.26). 'Why is the plural used? In order that men's successes may be attributed to God, but their failures may be laid on others. For it did not seem right to God to fashion with his own hand the downward inclination in man, wherefore he entrusted this portion of his work to his subordinate agents' (*De Conf. Ling.*, 35, 36).

(*d*) The Fall

The inevitable result of this attribution of the evil tendency to the creation of God was that men felt that they could blame God for their sins. That is why Ben Sirach breaks out:

> Say not, It is through the Lord that I fell away;
> For thou shalt not do the things that he hateth.
> Say not thou, It is he that caused me to err;
> For he hath no need of a sinful man. . . .
> He made man from the beginning,
> And left him in the hand of his own counsel.
> If thou wilt, thou shalt keep his commandments;

And to perform faithfulness is of thine own good pleasure.
He hath set fire and water before thee:
Thou shalt stretch forth thine hand unto whichsoever thou wilt.
Before man is life and death;
And whichsoever he liketh, it shall be given him

(Sirach 15.11-17).

And that is why James forbids a man to say that he is tempted
by God (James 1.13-15).

When Paul wrote Romans 5 all this was in his mind; but
there was more. In Romans 5 Paul makes much of the story of
the Fall in Genesis 3. In the rest of the Old Testament that story
has no influence; and in the New Testament, apart from the
writings of Paul, it plays no part. But we do find the germs of
Paul's use of it between the Testaments.

Ben Sirach writes:

> From a woman was the beginning of sin
> And because of her we all die
>
> *(Sirach 25.24).*

This is a first step toward the Pauline use of the story of the Fall;
but it must be noted that the word which is used for *beginning*
is *tehillah* which means *beginning* not in the causative but in the
temporal sense. This means that the act of Eve was 'the
beginning of the history of sin as far as man is concerned'.

Another step toward the Pauline use of the story of the Fall is
to be found in 4 Ezra. 4 Ezra combines the idea of the evil
tendency and of the permanent effect of the Fall. 'A grain of evil
seed was sown in the heart of Adam from the beginning, and
how much fruit of ungodliness has it produced unto this time,
and shall yet produce until the threshing-floor come' (4 Ezra
4.30). The permanent effect is spoken of in another passage:
'Then the first Adam, clothing himself with the evil heart,
transgressed and was overcome; and likewise also all who were

born of him. Thus the infirmity became inveterate; the Law indeed was in the heart of the people, but (in conjunction) with the evil germ; so what was good departed, and the evil remained' (4 Ezra 3.21-22). This writer breaks out despairingly: 'Better had it been that the earth had not produced Adam, or else, having once produced him (for thee), to have restrained him from sinning. . . . O thou Adam, what hast thou done! For though it was thou that sinned, the fall was not thine alone, but ours also who are thy descendants!' (4 Ezra 7.116-126). All the promises and all the gifts of Paradise and of the eternal age are as nothing if man is involved in futility and corruption and in the works which bring death because of the fall of Adam. In 4 Ezra the conception is that the sin of Adam brought something into the world which has involved all men in the darkness and the death of sin instead of the light and the glory of incorruption for which man was created. Just how this happened is not fully worked out – as it is in Paul – but the situation is decisively described.

Still one other of the books between the Testaments makes use of the story of Adam and of the Fall. In 2 Baruch the story occurs again. In it the idea is that the first sin of Adam brought death into the world and involved all men in physical death, but it did not necessarily involve man in sin.

> For though Adam first sinned
> And brought untimely death upon all,
> Yet of those who were born from him
> Each one of them has prepared for his own soul torment to come,
> And again each one of them has chosen for himself glories to
>   come. . . .
> Adam is therefore not the cause, save only of his own soul,
> But each of us has been the Adam of his own soul
>
> > *(2 Baruch 54.15-19).*

Here R. H. Charles comments: 'The evil impulse is not sin

unless obeyed. It is placed in man, say the Talmudists, to be overcome.'

It can be seen that the story of the Fall, although it had no influence on Old Testament thought, did exercise a very great influence on the thought of the writers between the Testaments. The way was prepared for Paul to use it. But Paul in his use of it was completely original. Oesterley points out that in the later Jewish theology, while Adam is universally regarded as the cause of the entry of death into the world, that happened, not so much because of his fall, as because of his refusal to show penitence for what he had done. 'When Adam transgressed the command of the Holy One, and ate of the tree, the Holy One demanded of him penitence, thereby revealing to him the means of freedom (from the result of his guilt). But Adam would not show penitence' (Midrash *Bemidbar Rabba*, xiii.). As we shall see, that is very different from the thought of Paul.

We have now seen the background and the heritage of thought into which Paul entered. It may be said that the materials of Pauline thought are there; but Paul was to make a new use of them, and what that use was we must now go on to see.

Paul's Two Problems

We have seen the place that the Adam story had in Jewish thought, and now we must go on to see the use which Paul made of it.

Paul has two problems to solve. First, how did sin and death get into the world and gain such a universal dominion over men? Second, how is it that Jesus Christ rescues men from that situation? As C. H. Dodd points out, the person to whom Paul preached might well say: 'I am quite prepared to accept the greatness of Jesus Christ. I accept him as a great, heroic, wise, prophetic figure. But he is one man, one single individual. How can that which one single individual has done possibly affect all mankind?' These are the questions which Paul sets out to answer in this passage.

The Adam Story

Paul twice in his Letters uses the Adam story. He uses it in a much more summary and simplified way in I Corinthians 15.21-22: 'Since by man came death, by man came also the resurrection of the dead. For as in Adam all die, even so in Christ shall all be made alive.' This is the principle which is more fully worked out in Romans 5.12-19. T. R. Glover (*Paul of Tarsus*, 25) speaks of 'the tangents that haunt Paul's writings', and says that these tangents 'show the sudden swiftness with which he pounces on a new idea or truth'. It is not strictly true to say that *vv.* 13-17 are a tangent, but they are a parenthesis as the A. V. correctly shows. The dilemma is stated in *v.* 12. It was by one man's sin that sin entered into the world. The whole thesis of the passage is stated in *v.* 18. Verse 18 is an extraordinarily telegraphic verse; there is not a verb in it from beginning to end. It reads almost like a skeleton mnemonic of the scheme of salvation: 'So then – as through one trespass – to all men – to condemnation – so also – through one righteous act – to all men – to justification of life'. To put it in one brief sentence – in Adam all men became sinners, in Jesus Christ all men became righteous. How, then, does Paul work this out!

We must begin from *v.* 12 – 'As by one man sin entered into the world, and death by sin; and so death passed upon all men, *eph' hō pantes hēmarton.* What is the meaning of the last phrase? In the phrase *eph' hō* is the *hō* masculine or neuter? If it is masculine the only possible antecedent must be *Adam*, who is, as it were, contained in the expression *one man*. The meaning will then be that sin and death entered into the world through one man in whom all sinned. This is the way in which

Bengel took it – '*omnes peccarunt Adamo peccante*'. If it is neuter, then the phrase will mean that sin and death entered into the world through one man, in that all sinned. In either case the meaning is the same; and in any event the important and significant matter is the tense of the verb *hēmarton*. That verb is an aorist. It means that sin and death entered into the world, not because all men *sin*, as it were habitually, but because all men *sinned*. Further, if we are to give the aorist tense its full value, and in this argument we must do so, the more precise meaning will be that sin and death entered into the world because all men were guilty *of one act of sin*. In *v.* 19 the matter is put in a different way – 'By one man's disobedience the many were constituted [*katestathēsan*] sinners'. It is to be noted that the Greek has the article before *many* – *hoi polloi* – a point which the R.S.V. misses, but which Moffat correctly takes, when he translates, 'Just as one man's disobedience made *all the rest* sinners'. The contrast is between the single individual Adam and the many, who are the rest of mankind. What, then, does Paul mean, when he says that in the one sinful act of Adam all mankind sinned, and by that one act all were constituted sinners? Four main explanations have been advanced.

(*a*) 'Every man is his own Adam'
It has been taken to mean that 'every man is his own Adam' (2 Baruch 54.19), that judgment and condemnation and death have come upon mankind, each man *for his own sin*. The Greek Fathers usually adopted this explanation. Theodoret comments: 'Not on account of his forefathers' sin, but on account of his own, each man received the doom of death'. Cramer in the *Catena* quotes Cyril who says that the meaning is that 'we have become imitators [*mimētai*] of the sin of Adam', and that sin spread through the world and mankind 'like an infection from a root'. This interpretation individualizes man's responsibility

for sin, and is, in fact, as we shall see, the precise opposite of the whole argument of Paul.

(*b*) Adam our representative

There is what is called the *legal* interpretation. It holds that Adam acted, not for himself alone, but as the *representative* of the human race, and that naturally, correctly and inevitably the human race is involved in the responsibility for the action of their representative. The objection to this view is that a representative cannot be in any real sense a representative, unless he is *chosen* by those whom he represents. This is certainly not the case with Adam, and to make people responsible for the actions of a representative with whose choice they had nothing to do is intolerably unjust.

(*c*) Inherited tendency to sin

There is the interpretation which suggests that what mankind inherited from Adam was the *tendency* to sin. Cramer in the *Catena* cites Gennadius as saying that what man inherited was Adam's *nature*. The result of this is that theoretically man has freedom of choice, and need not sin, unless he chooses to do so; but practically, and in point of fact, sin is inevitable because man's inherited nature is such as it is. From the Jewish point of view, we might express this by saying that the evil tendency, the *yēṣer ha-ra'*, is the nature which mankind inherited from Adam, and that it makes man's sin inevitable. From the modern point of view, we might express this by saying that, because of his heredity, man is inevitably predisposed to sin.

(*d*) Adam's descendants sinned in Adam

To the mind of a modern man the third of these interpretations is undoubtedly the most acceptable; but equally undoubtedly it is not what Paul meant. So we come to the fourth interpretation, which is called the *realistic* interpretation. According to this interpretation the meaning of this passage is that quite literally all Adam's descendants sinned in Adam; that they sinned in Adam's sin; that they literally committed an act of sin, when Adam disobeyed and sinned. There is a very close parallel to this kind of thought in the Letter to the Hebrews. The author is seeking to establish that the priesthood after the order of Melchizedek is the supreme priesthood, greater than any existing priesthood. We are told in Scripture that Abraham paid tithes to Melchizedek. In Jewish religious law it was to the tribe of Levi, to the Levites, that tithes were paid. But when Abraham paid tithes to Melchizedek, Levi, though still unborn, was in the loins of Abraham; and, therefore, in Abraham the yet unborn Levi paid tithes to Melchizedek, which means that the tribe whose right it is to receive tithes actually paid tithes to Melchizedek, a fact which establishes the unique supremacy of the priesthood after the order of Melchizedek (Hebrews 7.5-10). Here, then, Levi is literally credited with an action which took place before he was born.

Paul's basic contention is that all men literally and really sinned in Adam. Man is not only, so to speak, a sinner in his own individual right; Adam is not simply the representative of mankind; it is not simply the tendency to sin which man inherited from Adam; every individual man sinned in the sin of Adam, and is personally involved in that sin. Behind Paul's conclusions there lie two general principles, without which he could not have arrived at his conclusions.

Behind the whole argument there lies the principle of *solidarity*. The modern Western mind has become so used to thinking in terms of the individual that for it the idea of solidarity is difficulty to grasp. In early and in primitive times men tended to think of themselves, not as individuals, but as members of a clan, or family, or group. Apart from the group their lives have no meaning or significance. They do not exist as individuals, and they do not think of themselves as individuals; they think of themselves always as being indissolubly bound up within the group. It is said that, if an Australian aborigine is asked his name, he will begin by giving, not his own name, but the name of his tribe. This idea of solidarity is part and parcel of Jewish thought at all times.

We see it dramatically exemplified in the story of Achan (Joshua 7). The children of Israel had taken Jericho, but the condition of its capture had been that no man should keep any of the spoils for himself, and that everything in the city should be totally destroyed except the vessels of silver and gold and brass and iron, which must be consecrated to the treasury of the Lord (Joshua 6.17-19). Achan had disobeyed this condition, and had taken for himself a goodly Babylonish garment, two hundred shekels of silver, and a wedge of gold of fifty shekels weight. At the time Achan's disobedience was not known. The Israelites moved on to deal with Ai. It was reported that Ai was so insignificant that a small force was sufficient to capture it. But in the campaign against Ai Israel suffered a serious and humilitating setback and defeat. It was clear that in some way the nation had offended against God. The guilty party had to be found. On God's instruction Joshua took the people tribe by tribe, household by household and family by family. By a process of elimination Achan was discovered. He admitted his sin. He and his whole family, his sons and his daughters, were taken to the valley of Achor, and first stoned, and then burned to death. Here the principle of solidarity is demonstrated. The whole nation was involved in, and affected by, the sin of Achan. When it came to a matter of punishment, not only was Achan punished; his whole family was wiped out along with him as a group.

Given this principle of solidarity, it is possible to see why the whole human race is involved in the sin of Adam. Adam and all his descendants are bound up in one, and what the head of the family did the whole family did in him, and the whole family is equally responsible.

The second principle which lies behind Paul's whole argument is the connection of death with sin. Adam was created for immortality; Adam sinned and lost his immortality. The belief is that if there is no sin there is no death, and death is the direct consequence of sin.

The Steps in Paul's Argument

Let us now set out the steps of the argument in which Paul demonstrates the fact that in Adam all men sinned.

1. Adam sinned by a direct act of disobedience to an expressed command of God (*v.* 12), and because of that sin, death came to Adam.

2. Between Adam and Moses the law did not exist, for the law was not given until it was given to Moses. If there is no law, there can be no breach of the law, and, therefore, there can be no such thing as sin. Sin is not reckoned against a man when there is no law (*v.* 13).

3. In spite of the fact that there was no law, and, therefore, no debiting of sin between Adam and Moses, men continued to die. Those who had not sinned in the way in which Adam sinned nevertheless still died. The Greek is that death came *epi tous mē hamartēsantas epi tō homoiōmati tēs parabaseōs Adam* (*v.* 14). It is clear that for certain of the copyists the argument was as difficult as it is for us, for in certain manuscripts the *mē* (not) is missed out; and the statement becomes a statement that death came to those who *had* sinned in the way as Adam sinned, which is exactly what Paul does not say.

4. But if death is the direct cause of sin, which is disobedience to the law, and if between Adam and Moses there

was no law, and, therefore, no possibility of disobedience to the law, *why was it that men died*? The answer is – they died because they had sinned in Adam. Here is the proof that all men are involved in the sin of Adam. The undeniable fact that men still died under a dispensation when there was no law to break is for Paul the proof that all men are involved in the sin of Adam, and sinned in him. They inherited death because in Adam they sinned.

The Law Increased the Sin

So, then, by the sin of Adam all men were constituted sinners. At this point we must take in another Pauline idea, which comes at the end of the passage, but which for its place in the argument must be included here. Between Adam and Moses there was no law as yet given; but with Moses the law came; and, says Paul, 'the law entered that the offence might abound' (*v.* 20). Here, indeed, is a startling statement. How can the law be responsible for the *increase* of sin? There is more than one answer to that question.

1. The law necessarily makes a man aware of sin. When he receives the law he becomes conscious of the things which are sins, and of himself as a sinner. To put it another way, the law defines sin.

2. There is, therefore, a sense in which the law creates sin. To take a simple and imperfect analogy – it may be perfectly permissible for a long time to drive a motor car up or down a certain street, and to commit no crime. A new traffic regulation is approved, and that street then becomes a one-way street. By that new law a new breach of the law is there and then created, and there is one more crime which it is possible for a man to commit. Once the law comes, it defines sin, and in defining sin, it creates sin, for it renders illegal acts against which previously there was no law.

3. But there is a still more serious sense in which the law increases sin. It is a fact of human experience that once a thing is forbidden it develops a fatal fascination and attraction. That is exactly the situation which Paul personally knew so well. The commandment created desire; the command came and sin revived; sin took occasion by the commandment (Romans 7.7-11). Human nature being what it is, the fact that a thing is forbidden by the law thereby gives to that thing a new desirability.

But how can we say that the law was given *in order that* sin might abound and increase? Augustine here presents us with a helpful analogy (Augustine, on Psalm 102.15): 'In this God acted not with cruelty, but for the purpose of healing. For sometimes a man thinks himself whole, and is sick; and, inasmuch as he is sick and perceives it not, he seeks not a physician; but the disease is increased, the inconvenience grows, the physician is sought, and all is healed.' The idea is that the law made sin so acute, and the situation so desperate, that men are compelled to seek the remedy which only God can give.

Here, then, is the situation in which man is involved. By Adam's sin every man is constituted a sinner. Even if a man is a saint, he is none the less a sinner. Even if a man had committed no sin in his own person, he would still be a sinner. That is what the doctrine of original sin means. Further, the coming of the law has made matters worse, and has still more inextricably involved man in sin. Here is a literally desperate and hopeless situation. Man is inescapably involved in sin.

God sent his Son
In a situation like that only God can find a solution; and God found that solution by sending his Son into the world in the form of a man. Here a new factor enters the situation. In Jesus Christ, who is perfectly man, mankind makes a new beginning. Adam by his disobedience sinned, and thus rendered all men

sinners. Jesus Christ by his perfect obedience conquered sin, and thus opened to all men the possibility of righteousness. Men were constituted sinners in the man Adam; men can be constituted righteous in the new man Jesus Christ.

The Permanent Value of the Passage

Here, then, is the conception which Paul lays down in his passage. What are we to say of it, and wherein lies its permanent value?

It may well be that it is a mistake to treat this passage as theology at all. Paul was confronted with two things – the utter hopelessness of man in a Christless life; and the complete recreation of life in a Christ-filled life; and to express this double situation he uses this picture. T. R. Glover wrote of Paul (*Paul of Tarsus*, 109): ' "The depths of God" it is Paul's life-work and supreme interest to explore; he does not exhaust them. One of the reasons why Paul has been so inadequately studied of late years is that he was for long construed as a final authority, and his writings taken as a compendium of Theology, while his own idea was that he was a learner.' We would do well to remember that Paul did not write this passage as theology; he wrote it as a pictorial attempt to express the human situation, and how Christ altered that situation. If Paul's picture is pressed with literalness, it fails.

It involves accepting the story of the Fall as literal, factual history, and there are comparatively few who would be willing to take that definite step.

It confuses two kinds of relationships. Even if we take the story of the Fall literally, our connection with Adam is very different from our connection with Jesus Christ. In that case our connection with Adam is something which we cannot help; no man has anything to do with who his ancestors are; our connection with Adam is a purely physical relationship which we cannot by any means avoid or alter. On the other hand our connection with Jesus Christ is very different; it is something which we can accept or refuse. Jesus Christ is not our ancestor; he is the free gift of God to men (*vv.* 15,16). Our connection with him is not a physical connection; it is a connection of grace (*vv.* 15, 20, 21). Even as Paul himself tacitly admits, the fact that in Adam we are constituted sinners is a universal situation which no man can avoid simply because he is a man; the fact that we can become righteous, through our connection with Christ is a possibility which some through faith will accept, and others through unfaith will reject. The fact is that there is no true parallel between a man's connection with Adam and his connection with Jesus Christ. If there were a true connection, then the obedience of Jesus Christ would make all men righteous as automatically as the sin of Adam made all men sinners. Adam's sin gave men a status which no man could avoid; Jesus Christ's obedience opens to men a status, which every man must claim in faith.

But, even when we have made our criticisms, there remains eternal value in the picture which Paul here paints.

Seldom have the human dilemma and man's total helplessness to solve it been more powerfully presented. It remains true that man is a sinner, powerless to deal with his own sin apart from Jesus Christ. The human situation is a hopeless situation without God's entry into it in Jesus Christ.

Seldom has any thinker taken the Incarnation with such seriousness as Paul takes it here. The only thing which could rescue the human situation was God's identifying himself with that situation in Jesus Christ. And it is worth noting the effect of Paul's picture on any thinking about the Incarnation. In Paul's thinking Jesus Christ, in order to rescue man, had to be as fully man as Adam was; his identity with men had to be complete. Further, in Paul's thinking the life of Christ must be given an importance on an equality with the death of Christ. As an antidote to the disobedience of Adam Jesus Christ brings to God the perfect obedience. It is true that the culminating act of that obedience was the death of Christ, but that death would have been without value apart from the life of obedience which led up to it.

The supreme value of Paul's thought in this passage is the way in which it completely identifies Jesus Christ with mankind and with the human situation and with every man. Turgeniev has a story of a lad who was in church one day. As he listened to the story of Jesus Christ, he longed to see Christ, as it were, with his very own eyes. A man came and sat beside him; and there came to the lad the conviction that the man beside him was none other than Jesus himself. He was quite certain that this was he. And in his certainty he turned and looked, and to his intense surprise he saw that Jesus had 'a face like all men's faces'. We may criticise Paul's analogies and Paul's arguments; we may find his presuppositions strange and alien to our way of thought; the fact remains that he leaves us with the supreme truth that God rescued man by identifying himself with man in Jesus Christ.

4
Acts 2.14-40:
The First Christian Sermon

It would scarcely be an exaggeration to claim that Acts is the most important history book in the world, for without it we would know nothing about the history of the Early Church and the beginnings of the Christian religion, apart from what we could deduce and piece together from the letters of Paul. And within Acts this passage which we are about to study must rank high in interest, for it is the record of the first sermon preached in the Christian Church.

An Accurate Report?

No sooner have we said that than we face a problem, which we cannot evade, and about which there will be no unanimous agreement. In this and in other speeches in Acts have we an accurate and reliable account of what the preachers and speakers really said? Are Luke's versions of these sermons and speeches to be accepted as something in the nature of verbatim reports? Or, are they to be regarded as inventions or compositions by Luke himself? Or, are they to be regarded as based on sound tradition, although edited by Luke and stamped with the impress of his mind and style?

The factor which makes this so real a question is the ancient method of writing history. Ancient historians had a habit of liberally intermingling their narrative with speeches. In every crisis of history, when great decisions had to be taken, or great issues were at stake, the ancient historians supplied a speech by one of the chief actors in events. In the thirty-five extant books of Livy's history there are about four hundred speeches. One third of the history of Dionysius of Halicarnassus consists of speeches, and one fifth of the history of Thucydides. And none of these historians even pretended that the speeches which they inserted into their histories had any real connection with anything which was actually said.

The supreme master of the historical speech was Thucydides, and the standard exposition and examination of them is that by R. C. Jebb in the volume of essays entitled *Hellenica*. Thucydides sets out his own method in the speeches: 'As to the various speeches made on the eve of the war, or in its course, I have found it difficult to retain a memory of the precise words which I had heard spoken, and so it was with those who brought me reports. But I have made the persons say what it seemed to me most opportune for them to say in view of each situation; at the same time I have adhered as closely as possible to the general sense of what was actually said. As to the deeds done in war, I have not thought myself at liberty to record them on hearsay from the first informant, or on arbitrary conjecture. My account rests either on personal knowledge, or on the closest possible scrutiny of each statement made by others. The process of research was laborious, because conflicting accounts were given by those who had witnessed the several events, as partiality swayed or memory served them' (Thucydides, i. 21). Thucydides is perfectly frank about the method he followed. In regard to events he followed a policy of meticulous sifting and scrutinizing of his sources; in regard to the speeches he allowed himself free composition, based on what it was appropriate for the speaker to say, and on any reminiscences of the speech which were available. He certainly never intended the speeches to be taken as verbatim reports. In his essay on how history ought to be written Lucian lays down the principle: 'If ever it is necessary to introduce any one who will deliver an address, see to it that the words are specially appropriate to the character of the speaker and relevant to the situation; further, that they are as clear as possible. But at such a time you are permitted to play the orator, and to exhibit your rhetorical skill' (Lucian, *On How History Should Be Written*, 58). To Lucian historical speeches were essays in rhetoric rather than results of research.

The situation was in actual practice more serious than that. Few historians confined themselves within the limits of the restraint and moderation of the principles of Thucydides. Even when the original speeches were available, they still preferred to put into the mouths of the speakers speeches which were their own compositions and inventions. The speech of Caesar to his soldiers is quite different in the history of Dio Cassius (xxxviii. 30-46) from Caesar's own version of it (*B.G.*, i. 40). The speech of Claudius as reported by Tacitus (*Annals*, ii. 24) is quite different from the version on the original brass tablet found at Lyons (*Corpus Inscript. Latin.*, xiii. 1668). Moreover, from the literary point of view, it was these speeches which were reckoned the outstanding parts of the histories. Demosthenes studied the speeches in the history of Thucydides, and Quintilian praised those in the history of Livy. Even a Jewish historian like Josephus largely adopted this practice. Josephus, for instance, provides a long speech by Potiphar's wife when she had failed to seduce Joseph (Josephus, *Antiquities*, II. iv. 3-5).

The only ancient historian who repudiated this custom was Polybius. 'Surely', he writes, 'an historian should not aim at producing speeches which might have been delivered, nor study dramatic propriety in details like a writer of tragedy; but his function is above all to record with fidelity what was actually said or done, however commonplace it may be. For the purpose of history and drama are not the same' (Polybius, ii. 56). He

severely censures Timaeus because he did not set down the
actual words of speeches, or even the drift of them, but
'imagining how they ought to have been expressed, he
enumerates all the arguments used, like a schoolboy declaiming
on a set theme' (Polybius, xii. 25a). R. C. Jebb quotes Voltaire:
'Set speeches are a sort of oratorical lie, which the historian
used to allow himself in old times. He used to make his heroes
say what they might have said. . . . At the present day these
fictions are no longer tolerated. If one put into the mouth of a
prince a speech which he had never made, the historian would
be regarded as a rhetorician.'

All this presents us with a very real problem, and a problem
which we must solve before we can speak of our present passage
as the first recorded sermon of the Christian Church. Did Luke
follow the normal historical convention of his day and
generation, and are the speeches and sermons in Acts no more
than Luke's composition and free invention? Or, had Luke
sources and traditions which he followed, and are we entitled to
regard the speeches and sermons as trustworthy and reliable
accounts of what was said on the occasions which they
represent? Few would go so far as to claim that they are verbatim
reports. It would be impossible for any one to deny that Luke
edited them, and left the impress of his own style on them all.
But do they at least give the substance of what was said?

Two Differing Views

There are many scholars who believe that Luke was following
the normal convention of his age. Foakes-Jackson writes: 'The
student of classical literature will find it difficult to believe that
they are not compositions of the writer' (*Acts*, p. xvi). Jülicher
regards them as free inventions. If they fit the occasion, if Peter
is more Judaistic in his alleged speeches than Paul, if Paul's
alleged material differs to suit the occasion, that proves no more

than that Luke had good literary taste and sound historical imagination. After all, no other Christian was present during Paul's speech at Athens, nor at his private conversations with Felix, Festus, and Agrippa. Where then could any record have come from? (*Introduction to the New Testament*, Eng. tr., 443, 444). H. J. Cadbury concludes; 'The elaborate, homogeneous and schematic speeches suggest, if not the rhetoric, at least the free composition of the speeches in the Greek and Roman historians' (*Beginnings of Christianity*, ii. 15). True, this does not take everything away, for even then it can be held that the speeches 'indicate at least what seemed to a well-informed Christian of the next generation the main outline of the Christian message as first presented by Jesus' followers in Palestine and in the cities of the Mediterranean world' (*Beginnings of Christianity*, v. 247).

Is the evidence for such a view such that we cannot do other than agree to it, or, are there reasons which entitle us to go beyond that view? F. H. Chase in *The Credibility of the Book of the Acts of the Apostles* does present a case for going further; and in what follows we use and add to his arguments.

In New Testament times it would never be safe to say what could and what could not be remembered. It must never be forgotten that in those days the printed book did not exist, and that manuscript rolls were scarce and expensive, and that, therefore, if a man wished to possess a poem, a speech, or a story he had to remember it. Xenophon's Niceratus says: 'My father, wishing me to grow up into a good man, made me learn all the lines of Homer; and now I can repeat the whole of the *Iliad* and the *Odyssey* from memory' (Xenophon, *Symposium*, iii. 5). It is what Chase calls 'a supercilious forgetfulness' which fails to remember that the ancients were not altogether without certain modern accessories. Shorthand certainly existed, and Galen (xix. 11 [ed. Kuhn]) tells us that his medical students took down his lectures in some kind of shorthand. Note-taking is not a modern achievement. It is to be remembered that the East is 'naturally meditative', and the sermons and speeches of the leaders of the Early Church would be turned over and over in the mind. The Jew made much more than the Greek of the actual wording of teaching as the essential vehicle of the thought of the speaker, and would be much more likely to remember it. It is of first-class importance to remember that whatever tradition is behind the speeches and sermons, if there is one, would be a communal tradition. It would certainly not be a case of material being dependent on the memory of one or two persons; the memory behind it is the memory of the Church. And further, the sermons and speeches of the leaders of the Church were not something to be listened to, but something to be acted upon, and must, therefore, have been stored in the memory and repeatedly discussed. It is a matter of fact that a man does not readily forget the sermon by which he was converted.

It is not without significance, as Chase points out, that the sermons of Peter in Acts are curiously Jewish. The phrase 'the whole house of Israel' occurs nowhere else in the New Testament, but is part of the Jewish *Kaddish* prayer (Acts 2.36). Acts 3.13 is actually the first phrase of the great Jewish prayer, the *Shemoneh Esreh*, which a devout Jew prayed three times a day. 'Sons of the covenant' in Acts 3.25 is a characteristically Jewish phrase. If this is all invention, it is very subtle invention indeed. A feature of Acts is the difference between the Western and the Neutral texts, and it is a fact that the difference between these two texts is least in the speeches.

At for sources, for Paul's speeches Luke had Paul himself, and for the others, though he cannot have heard them, he must have been in close contact with many who did. Torrey's theory that behind Acts 1.1-15.36 there lies an Aramaic original source has not found universal acceptance, but it is a notable fact that most of the alleged Aramaisms in fact come from the speeches, which would seem to show that they do have an Aramaic source behind them.

We believe that the conclusion must be that the speeches in Acts are not entirely free compositions and rhetorical inventions by Luke, but that, though edited by him, and though no doubt owing much to his hand, they do go back to a sound and reliable tradition, and that, therefore, in the case of our present passage we are justified in regarding it as containing the substance of the first recorded sermon in the Christian Church.

A Message from God

It may well be that Luke underlines the importance of Peter's sermon by the word with which he introduces it. He says that Peter lifted up his voice and *said* unto them. The Greek for *said* is *apephthenxato*. This word occurs in only two other places in the New Testament, in Acts 2.4, where it describes the utterance of the Christians under the influence of the Holy Spirit, and in Acts 26.25 where Paul claims before Agrippa and Festus that he is *speaking forth* the words of truth and soberness. It is used of plainly staining one's opinion; but, more, it is used of the memorable utterances of wise men and philosophers; it is used of oracular utterances (Lucian, *Alexander*, 25); it is used by Vettius Valens in close conjunction with *maniōdēs* and *ekstatikos* (see Moulton and Milligan, *Vocabulary of the Greek Testament*). The Grimm-Thayer *Lexicon* lays it down that the word 'belongs to dignified and elevated discourse', and Arndt and Gingrich give it as 'the word of the wise man, the oracle-giver, the diviner, the prophet, the exorcist, and other "inspired" persons'. There is little doubt that Luke chose this word to indicate that an apostolic sermon – as every sermon ought to be – was not the expression of one man's opinions, but the utterance of a message from God mediated by the Holy Spirit. What, then, is this message and announcement of Peter?

Something has happened

It begins with the joyous announcement that something has happened, something which is the fulfilment of the hopes and dreams and expectations of the prophets. The Jews saw time divided into two ages. There was *this present age*, which was wholly bad, and wholly under the domination of evil, and there was *the age to come*, which was to be wholly good, the golden age, the age of God and of his kingdom. How was the one age to change into the other? That change could not come by human effort and human reformation; it could only come by the direct intervention and the direct action of God. The day on which God would intervene was known as the Day of the Lord. In effect, Peter says: The Day of the Lord has come; eternity has invaded time; God has acted; the old order has ended and the new order has begun. To prove his point and his assertion Peter quotes from Joel 2.28-32. That which the prophet has dreamed of and foretold has found its fulfilling. The events of Pentecost are that very outpouring of the Spirit which the prophet foretold. It may well be that Peter saw the fulfilment of the prediction that the sun would be turned into darkness and the moon into blood in the murky darkness which came upon Jerusalem during the Crucifixion (Matthew 27.45, Mark 15.33, Luke 23.44).

The variations in the text of the quotation make a fascinating and a most suggestive study. First, there are the alterations made, according to the Neutral Text, in the quotation. In Joel the passage begins *after these things* (*kai estai meta tauta*), that is, after the terrible plague of locusts described in the earlier part of the chapter. B retains this reading; but the other main uncials agree that Peter altered this into *in the last days* (*estai en tais eschatais hēmerais*). That is to say, Peter by this slight but definite alteration makes it clear that he sees in Jesus Christ and in the events of Pentecost the last times, the inbreak of God, the emergence of the new age. Further, the words *and they shall prophesy* in *v.* 18 are not part of the Joel quotation, and are, indeed, omitted in D. This stressing of this outbreak of prophecy, and this universalizing of the ability to prophesy is very significant. There is a midrash on Psalm 14.6 (57 b): 'Rabbi Levi said. . . . the Master is God who said, "O that they had such a heart as to fear me" (Deuteronomy 5.29); the pupil is Moses who said, "O that all the Lord's people were prophets" (Numbers 11.29); but neither the words of the Master nor of the Pupil find fulfilment in this world, but in the future the words of both will find fulfilment, the words of the Master for "I will give you a new heart" (Ezekiel 36.26), and the words of the Pupil for "I will pour out my spirit upon all flesh" (Joel 2.28)'. This is to say that only in the heavenly age would this gift of universal prophecy come to men. The very stressing of the universality of the prophetic gift is another claim that heaven has invaded earth in the coming of Jesus and the descent of his Spirit.

But in some ways the alterations of the Western Text in D are even more significant. The Neutral Text is that God will pour out his spirit *epi pasan sarka*, on all flesh; D has *epi pasas sarkas* literally, on all fleshes. Further, instead of *hoi huioi kai hai thugateres humōn*, your sons and your daughters, D has *hoi huioi autōn kai hai thugateres autōn*, i.e., their sons and daughters. Of the purpose of this there is no doubt. It is to remove the last vestiges of nationalism from the prophecy, and to insist that the promise was made to the whole wide world, and that in Jesus Christ the promise to the whole wide world has been fulfilled.

The first sentence of the actual message of the first Christian sermon was the affirmation that something has happened. It is not the hope that something will happen, not even the promise of things to come. It is the statement that the last days have come, that eternity has broken in on time, that God has acted as he always said that he would act, that the promised Messianic age has come. Things which are possible only in the heavenly age are happening; the Messianic events are unfolding themselves before the very eyes of men. And further, even at the very beginning, there were implications which at the moment were not seen, but which were bound to work themselves out. There was the implication that any bonds which limited the promises of God to some most favored nation were burst and broken, and that, as the Western Text even labors to underline, this outpouring of Divine life is for all men of all nations. It is well to remember that the Christian preaching began with the announcement of an act of God for all men.

History has a Purpose and a Direction

We may here note another fact about the beginning of this first sermon. It is of the greatest significance that the sermon opens with a quotation from prophecy, and that it continues to use prophecy all the way through. It may be that the citation and the quotation of prophecy is nowadays a method of presenting the Christian message which for many has lost its impressiveness. But the very fact that there can be such a thing as prophecy indicates a certain view of history. If there can be such a thing as prophecy, it necessarily means that in history there is plan and purpose, that history is not a meaningless succession of chance and unrelated events, but that it is going somewhere, and is under some direction.

The Stoics believed that history was an eternal repetition of the same things. Chrysippus sets out the theory that at certain fixed periods of time there comes a universal conflagration which destroys the cosmos, and then everything begins again in precisely the same way. 'Socrates and Plato and each individual man will live again, with the same friends and fellow-citizens. They will go through the same experiences and the same activities . . . And this restoration of the universe takes place not

once, but over and over again – to all eternity without end . . .
There will never be any new thing other than that which has
been before, but everything is repeated to the minutest detail.'
History to the Stoic was an ever-repeated cycle from which
there is no escape. G. N. Clark in his Inaugural Lecture at
Cambridge insisted that there is no secret and no plan
discoverable in history. 'I do not believe that any future
consummation could make sense of all the irrationalities of the
preceding ages. If it could not explain, still less could it justify
them.' Herbert Fisher said: 'Men wiser and more learned than
myself have discerned in history a plot, a rhythm, a pre-
determined pattern. I can see only one emergency following
upon another, as wave follows upon wave.' André Maurois
wrote: 'The universe is indifferent. Who created it? Why are we
here on this puny mud heap spinning in infinite space? I have
not the slightest idea, and I am convinced that no one has the
slightest idea.'

There are many voices to proclaim what they believe to be
the senselessness of history. The very fact that the first Christian
sermon begins with a quotation from prophecy is the
affirmation of faith that behind the kaleidoscope of events there
is the unfolding purpose of God.

It has happened through Jesus
We have seen that this first Christian sermon begins with the
joyful announcement that something has happened, that
eternity has broken into time, that the end time has come, and
that the great prophetic promises have been fulfilled. There
follows an equally emphatic announcement, the announcement
that this has happened through the life, the death, and the
resurrection of Jesus. To many the supreme interest of this
passage will lie in its Christology, for here is the Christology, not
of men who thought about Jesus as a theological figure, but who

had never seen him, but of men who had known him, walked with him, talked with him in the days of his flesh, of men who had seen him live, who had watched him die, and who had met him when he rose again.

(*a*) A man approved of God

Peter describes Jesus in the most startling way. 'Jesus of Nazareth', he says, 'a man approved of God among you by miracles and wonders, and signs, which God did by him in the midst of you' (*v.* 22). The extraordinary feature of this description of Jesus is its heaping up of human terms. The name is Jesus, not Jesus Christ, not the Lord Jesus, simply Jesus. He is localized as coming from Nazareth, a definite and identifiable Galilean place. He is bluntly and uncompromisingly called a man (*andra*). He is *approved* by God. Here there is a variant reading which is of the greatest interest and significance. The reading of the Neutral Text, and of all the best manuscripts, with one exception, is *apodedeigmenon*, which is reflected in Tertullian's *destinatum* (Tertullian, *Pud.*, xxi.; cf. *Res. Carn.*, xv.). But the reading of the Western Text is *dedokimasmenon*, which is reflected in Irenaeus' *adprobatum* (Irenaeus, *Adv. Haer.*, III. xii. 2), and in certain old Latin manuscripts. Let us inquire into the meaning of these two very important words.

First, let us look at the verb *apodeiknumi*. At its simplest it can be used of pointing at something in order to direct attention to it. Thucydides used it for *pointing* at the sepulchres of common ancestors (Thucydides, i. 26). It can be used of bringing forward proofs that something is true (Herodotus, v. 45). It can be used of appointing or assigning an altar to a divinity (Herodotus, v. 178). It can be used of advancing an argument (Thucydides, ii. 72), or of demonstrating by argument that some one is something. Euripides, for instance, uses it of demonstrating that some one is a traitor (Euripides, *Ion*, 879).

When it is used more directly of persons it can mean to appoint, to proclaim, or to create. It can be used of appointing a commander (Herodotus, i. 124); a general (Herodotus, i. 162); a captain of the horse (Herodotus, vii. 154). It can be used of putting some one into a certain condition, for instance, of an officer producing such conditions of discipline and service that he puts his platoon of soldiers into the best possible condition (Xenophon, *Cyropaedia*, II. i. 23). It can be used of representing some one as something (Herodotus, i. 136). It can be used of ordaining a person to a certain state. Xenophon says that the Spartan law-giver ordained that the coward who did not keep the code should no longer be reckoned amongst the peers (Xenophon, *Constit. Lac.*, x. 7).

Moulton and Milligan cite the following uses of it. It is used of nominating an heir to an estate, of appointing supervisors, of establishing a title to ownership. And it can be used of appointing a person as Emperor. It is said on the accession of Nero to the imperial power: 'The expectation and hope of the world has been declared emperor.' *Hupatos apodedeigmenos* is the regular phrase for consul designate.

In general, then, the word means to appoint, to designate to an office.

Let us now look at *dokimazo*, the word of the variant reading of the Western Text. It can mean 'to put to the test'. Thucydides uses it for testing the reliability of witnesses (Thucydides, vi. 53), and Xenophon uses it of testing the reality of a man's friendship (Xenophon, *Mem.*, II, vi. 1). It can be used of that which is approved and attested by usage, custom and experience as contrasted with that which is novel and untried (Thucydides, ii. 35). It is commonly used of approving some one for an office after due scrutiny and examination. Plato uses it of the scrutiny of State officials prior to their appointment to office (Plato, *Laws*, 765 B); Aristotle uses it for the scrutiny of the qualifications of councilors (Aristotle, *Constit. Ath.*, xlv. 3). It is used of passing a cavalryman as fit for service (Xenophon, *Anab.*, III. iii. 20), and Aristotle uses it of the admission of boys to the ranks of the *ephebi* (the youths of eighteen to twenty years of age who did national service in Athens), and of the admission of the *ephebi* to the status of manhood (Aristotle, *Constit, Ath.*, xlii. 2).

Moulton and Milligan show from the papyri that the word comes to be a technical term for passing the tests necessary for any office. It is used of a magistrate sifting evidence; of inspecting animals for sacrifice; of arbitrators appointed to settle some dispute and approved by both parties to the dispute. It is used of a physician who has passed his examination, who has stood the test of this knowledge of medical technique and who is approved in character.

It may be said that both words amount to very much the same thing, but that *dedokimasmenos* sharpens and accentuates the idea that is in *apodedeigmenos*. They both mean 'to appoint', 'to designate' to some office, especially after all the necessary tests and scrutiny.

The startling thing about this is that this is something very like that which later came to be known as an Adoptionist Christology, which held that Jesus was a man who was specially chosen, adopted, by God for his special purposes, because he had proved himself worthy of such a choice. If it be asked when that choice and adoption took place, the commonest and the simplest answer would be at his baptism. In Luke 3.22 we again meet with an interesting and significant variant reading. The verse gives us the words of the Divine voice at the baptism of Jesus. The consistent reading of the Neutral Text is: 'Thou art my beloved Son; in thee I am well pleased.' But the Western Text, and there is support from Justin, Clement Methodius, Ambrosiaster, Tyconius and Augustine, reads: 'Thou art my beloved Son; this day have I begotten thee', which is in fact a quotation from Psalm 2.7, and which again has an Adoptionist tinge and coloring.

The difficulty of this phrase for orthodoxy is seen in the many translations of it. Lake and Cadbury in *The Beginnings of Christianity* translate *appointed*; Moffatt and Weymouth have *accredited*; Kingsley Williams has *proclaimed*; Phillips has *proved to be*; R.S.V. has *attested*. The fact is that here we have the most primitive of all Christologies, and that Christology is Adoptionist. No one is going to deny that as the years went on and as men's minds wrestled with the problem of the Person of Christ that Christology was left far behind; and no one is going to claim that Adoptionism is an adequate explanation of Jesus Christ; but, before we anathematize such a Christology, it is well to remember that it has its place in the New Testament, and that it came first to the minds of at least some of those who had known Jesus in the days of His flesh.

(*b*) The Paradox of the Death of Jesus

Next, we must look at what Peter's sermon has to say about the death of Jesus. This is summed up in v. 23: 'This Jesus, delivered up according to the definite plan and foreknowledge of God, you crucified and killed by the hands of lawless men' (R.S.V.). There is in this verse the characteristic outlook of Acts on the death of Christ. Here, and all through the Book of Acts two convictions about the death of Jesus are joined together.

(*a*) It is unvaryingly held that the death of Jesus was part of the purpose and the plan of God. It was in 'the definite plan and foreknowledge of God'. God showed beforehand by the mouth of the prophets all that Christ should suffer, and these things have now been fulfilled (3.18). The Jews and Romans rose up to do against Christ 'whatsoever thy hand and thy counsel determined before to be done' (4.28). It was, says Paul, when they had fulfilled 'what was written of Christ' that they took him down from the tree (13.29). Acts is convinced that the sufferings and the death of Christ were part of the plan and the purpose of God. There is nothing of the idea that the Cross was a kind of emergency action which God had taken only when everything else had failed and gone wrong. There is no suggestion that things, so to speak, had got out of control. There is not the slightest tinge of any opposition between Jesus Christ and God, no hint of that kind of theology in which it may almost be said that a gentle and loving Jesus pacified a stern and angry God. The Cross was part of the eternal plan of God.

(*b*) But side by side with that in this passage, and everywhere in its thinking, Acts sees the Cross as the most terrible crime in history. The early preachers could not speak of the Cross without a shuddering thrill of horror in their voices. 'Ye denied the Holy One and the Just, and desired a murderer to be granted unto you; and killed the Prince of life' (3.14). 'Jesus Christ of Nazareth, whom ye crucified,' 'Jesus, whom ye slew and hanged on a tree' (4.10, 5.30) – the words are simple, but they are instinct with the feeling that here is a terrible and a tragic crime at the hands of men.

Here is the eternal paradox of the Cross; the Cross is at one and the same time the action of the purpose and the plan of the love of God, and an unspeakably terrible crime at the hands of wicked men. At first sight herein is a paradox and a contradiction. But it is the paradox which lies at the very heart of the human situation, because it sets side by side the Divine will of God and the mystery of the free will of man. The Cross must always remain at one and the same time the act of God's love and the crime of man's sin.

(*c*) The Resurrection – God's Great Act

Next Peter goes on to affirm the Resurrection, and it is of the

greatest significance that Peter spends more time (vv. 24-31) on
the Resurrection than on anything else. Acts is characteristically
the Gospel of the Risen Christ. Once again the Resurrection is
guaranteed by the citation of prophecy; Psalm 16.8-11 is
worked out as a foretelling of the Resurrection. For the disciples
themselves the Resurrection was 'the star in the firmament of
Christianity'. It was to it they owed their faith. The Cross had
left them broken and bewildered; it was the Resurrection which
gave them their faith. We have only to think of Peter before and
after the Resurrection. In the time of the Cross his faith
collapsed, fear conquered him, and he denied his Lord. After
the Resurrection this self-same Peter courageously defined the
same Sanhedrin which had sent his Lord to the Cross, and
which could send him to a like fate. Every effect must have an
adequate cause; and nothing but the Resurrection can explain
the astonishing change in the disciples.

But the most characteristic thought of Acts about the
Resurrection is that the Resurrection is the work of God.
'Whom God hath raised up', says Peter. 'This Jesus hath God
raised up' (*vv.* 24, 32). This is the characteristic statement of
Acts. You 'killed the Prince of life, whom God hath raised from
the dead' (3.15). 'Jesus Christ of Nazareth, whom ye crucified,
whom God raised from the dead' (4.10).

It may be that sometimes the Resurrection is presented as a
victory and a triumph of Jesus; it is not so in Acts; in Acts the
Resurrection is an act of God.

In Acts, and, indeed, in all New Testament thought, God is
behind everything. There is no danger of tritheism. There is no
danger of what H. Richard Niebuhr called 'Christism (*The
Purpose of the Church and its Ministry*, 44-47). The lonely
supremacy of God remains. The writers of the New Testament
were Jews, and were, therefore, uncompromisingly
monotheistic. The Resurrection is not the achievement even of

Jesus Christ; it is the Divine act of the power of God.

So Peter's thought about Jesus rises to its natural conclusion and culmination. The outcome of Jesus' life, the outcome of his death, and the outcome of his Resurrection is his exaltation (v. 33). Once again this is guaranteed by the appeal to prophecy, and the citation of Psalm 110.1. And it is this exaltation which gives Jesus Christ the right to make his unparalleled demands and to offer his unparalleled promises. It is this which proves him to be both Lord and Christ (v. 36). It is this which demonstrates him to be the promised and the awaited Messiah.

Two Demands and Two Promises
Once Peter has confronted his hearers with the fact of Jesus Christ and his Messiahship, and once his words have moved their hearts, he goes on to make two demands and offer two promises.

(1) Repent
He demands that they should *repent*. The Greek word for repentance is *metanoia*, and it is a word of the greatest interest. *Metanoia* literally means an *afterthought* as opposed to *pronoia* which means *forethought*. An afterthought, a second thought, is usually a changed thought. That is to say, it is a realization and an admission that the previous way and the previous action were wrong. To realize that the previous way was wrong ought to result in regret and sorrow for it. And, if that regret and sorrow have any reality, they ought to issue in a new way and in amendment of life. In all real repentance there must, then, be three elements – the realization of the wrongness of the past, sorrow for that wrongness, and the decision to amend life in the future. If any of these elements is lacking, repentance is incomplete. We may say that repentance involves a change of mind, a change of heart, and a change of life. It is nothing less

than that that Peter was demanding from his hearers – and that must still be the prophetic demand of the preacher.

(2) Be Baptized

There is the demand for *baptism* as entrance into the Christian Church. With this demand a Jew would be perfectly familiar, for baptism was in fact the way in which proselytes entered the Jewish faith. Baptism, sacrifice, so long as the Temple stood, and circumcision were the three necessary preliminaries to entry into the Jewish faith. But it is necessary to realize what baptism was and meant and implied at this stage of the Church. In the nature of things at this stage in the history of the Church baptism was adult baptism, and was the step by which a man professed his faith in Jesus Christ. Equally in the nature of things baptism was instructed baptism, and there were some in the Church who would have insisted that a man must undergo as much as seven years' instruction in the faith before he was baptized. Even in a passage like this, where baptism seems to follow almost immediately, those to be baptized still receive the word. Baptism, as indeed proselyte baptism was, was by real immersion, and it was by the sinking below the water and the rising from it again that unity with the death and the resurrection of Christ was symbolized – and more than symbolized. Finally, baptism was what might be called ethical baptism. It brought that to a man which enabled him to live a new life in which sin had no more power to lord it over him. The gateway to the Christian fellowship was the gateway of baptism.

(3) Forgiveness of Sins

Having made the demands, Peter offers the promises. There is the offer of *forgiveness of sins*. The word for forgiveness is *aphesis*, and the characteristic atmosphere of this word is *release*. It can describe all kinds of releases – the release of water to the fields when the Nile sluice-gates were opened; the release from debt and the remission of debt; the release from captivity; the release from some civic obligation which a citizen must perform. It is the freeing from a debt which a man cannot pay, and from an obligation which he cannot fulfil. What Peter was offering men through Jesus Christ was a new relationship with God in which a man no longer had the dreadful feeling of being in default and under condemnation for his failure in his duties and his obligations, a relationship in which the dread of God had become peace with God.

(4) Gift of Holy Spirit

Finally, the promise is the promise of the *Holy Spirit*. And in Acts the action of the Holy Spirit on the life of a man is such that all can see it (Acts 10.46, 19.6). Acts is the Gospel of the Holy Spirit, and in its first thirteen chapters there are more than forty references to the Holy Spirit. That which Peter was offering through Jesus Christ was release from the past and power for the future combined.

If not . . .

After the demands and the promises there comes, as it were, one last word 'Save yourselves from this untoward generation' (*v.* 40). That is to say that the Christian message ended with a threat. It bluntly confronted a man with the alternative of being saved or of perishing. The early preachers did not hesitate to tell men what would happen, if the offer of Christ was not accepted.

In *Grace Abounding* John Bunyan tells of the Sunday on which he heard a sermon on the Sabbath. On that same afternoon, he goes on, 'as I was in the midst of a game of cat, and having struck it one blow from the hole, just as I was about to strike it the second time a voice did suddenly dart from heaven into my soul, which said, "Wilt thou leave thy sins and go to heaven, or have thy sins and go to hell?" ' Here was the clear-cut alternative, and it was with that alternative that early preaching confronted its hearers.

The Pattern of the Early Preaching

Here, then, in this sermon of Peter, we have the main elements in early preaching, and we may now set them down that we may compare them with our own practice.

(1) First and foremost, it was the proclamation of an act of God, the announcement of the saving activity of God. It was not so much a debater's argument, however clever, as it was a witness's affirmation.

(2) It laid down the centrality of Jesus Christ in that action of God. It dealt with the life, the death, the resurrection, the exaltation and the Messiahship of Jesus, and its characteristic stress was even more on the Resurrection than it was on the Cross.

(3) It insisted that all history had pointed to Jesus Christ, and to the great events of his life. It laid particular stress and emphasis on the fulfilment of prophecy, and in so doing it witnessed to its belief in the purpose and the plan of God, and, therefore, in the purpose and the plan of history.

(4) It demanded repentance, and that repentance was not merely a comfortable, languishing, sentimental regret; it was not simply regret at the consequences and the results of sin; it was a complete change of mind, heart, and life, so complete a change that it could only be described in terms of a new man and a new life.

(5) It summoned to baptism as the gateway of entry into the Church, and the means of union with Christ, and washing from sin.

(6) It offered forgiveness for the past, remission of the debt and the obligation which a man had necessarily incurred to God; and, therefore, it offered a new relationship to God.

(7) It offered the gift of the Spirit through Jesus Christ, so that not only would the past be forgiven, but the future would be strengthened and renewed and directed.

(8) It uttered a stern warning of the consequence of neglecting this offer. To accept it is to be saved; to refuse it is to perish.

Such, then, was the pattern of the first preaching, and it is a pattern which is still the pattern to be copied.

5
Revelation 13:
The Mystery of the Beast

It may well be that more ink has been spilled over this chapter than over any other chapter in the New Testament. For all that, it still exercises the fascination of the mysterious, and it still provides material for both the study of the seeker and the ingenuity of the eccentric.

A New Attitude towards the State

The basic key to this chapter, and indeed to the whole of the Revelation, lies in the fact that in the Revelation we come face to face with an attitude to the State which is quite different from that of any other part of the New Testament. Jesus deliberately refused to be drawn into any statement which would indicate hostility to the State, or refusal to accept obligations to the State (Matthew 22.15-22, Mark 12.13-17, Luke 20.20-26). Paul was proud of his Roman citizenship (Acts 21.39, 22.25-28), and never hesitated to use the privileges which it conferred upon him. It was true that for Paul time and time again the fact that he was a citizen had saved him from insult and ill-treatment, and that for him the tribunal of the magistrate had been the place of protection from the fury of the mob. It had been so in Philippi (Acts 16), in Corinth (Acts 18), in Ephesus (Acts 19), and in Jerusalem (Acts 21 and 22). It had been Paul's view that the powers that be are ordained of God, and that the Christian must render a conscientious obedience to them (Romans

13.1-6). In the Pastoral Epistles it is laid down that prayer is to be made for kings and for all who are in authority (I Timothy 2.1). In I Peter the injunction is to be a good citizen, to be subject to governors, to fear God, and to honor the Emperor (I Peter 2.13-17). In II Thessalonians 2.6, 7 the most probable interpretation is that the Roman Empire is the power which alone restrains and postpones the advancing chaos of the end. There is nothing here of opposition or enmity to the State. The whole attitude is that the Christian must accept his obligations to, and the authority of, the State.

But, when we reach the Revelation, all this has changed. Rome is the supreme enemy, the incarnation of devilish and satanic power, the great harlot, the mother of abominations, drunk with the blood of the saints and the martyrs (Revelation 17.5, 6), doomed to divine destruction. It is indeed worth noting that Streeter (*The Primitive Church*, 133) regards I Peter as a deliberate correction of the Revelation. Streeter does not accept the Petrine authorship of I Peter, and he regards it as contemporary with the Revelation in the time of Domitian. He regards I Peter as written by a man who is inside the official structure of the Church and the Revelation as written by a man who is not. To the writer of the Revelation the civil power is on the side of Satan. 'In I Peter 4.12-5.11 we have the reaction from within of the man who is responsible for the Church. . . . He knows that it is dangerous to teach that kind of thing in a Levantine slum. Like Paul, he recognizes in the Roman Empire, with all its faults, a power that upholds law, order, and civil justice. He had himself, perhaps only a year or two earlier [Streeter sees I Peter as composed of two separate documents], urged his people to look on rulers as sent by God "for vengeance on evil-doers and for praise to them that do well". It is no longer possible for him to speak so. But he will still urge the Christians not to lose their heads (4.12f.); and, above all, not to come into conflict with the authorities in so far as they do function legitimately as the upholders of law and order.' It is not necessary to accept all Streeter's position to agree that the Revelation manifests a new hostility to the State which has no parallel in the rest of the New Testament. Whence, then, does this new opposition spring?

The basic background of the Revelation is Caesar-worship, and without some understanding of Caesar-worship it is not possible to understand the Revelation; and that is specially true of this chapter.

Caesar-worship

(*a*) Worship of Rome

Caesar-worship did not begin as Caesar-worship; it began as the worship of Rome. In the beginning it was not imposed on the people; it emerged from the people as an act of gratitude. It was especially strong in Asia Minor. E. J. Goodspeed (*An Introduction to the New Testament*, 240) writes: 'It was the glory of the Roman Empire that it brought peace to a troubled world. Under its sway the regions of Asia Minor and the East enjoyed tranquility and security to an extent and for a length of time unknown before and probably since. The provincial, under Roman sway, found himself in a position to conduct his business, provide for his family, send his letters, and make his journeys in security, thanks to the strong hand of Rome.' It was little wonder that men saw something divine in the spirit of Rome. The first temple to the spirit of Rome was erected in Smyrna in 195 B.C. (Tacitus, *Annals*, iv. 56). This worship of Rome went steadily on; we hear, for instance, in 98 B.C. of priests of Rome being present at a compact between Ephesus and Sardis.

(*b*) Rome personified in the emperor

But worship of the goddess Roma is not yet Caesar-worship. The actual worship of the Emperor arose from two circumstances. First, there is the quite general fact that the worship of Roma was the worship of an abstraction, the spirit of Rome; and that abstraction was personalized and incarnated in the person of the Emperor. It was easier to worship the incarnation of the spirit of Rome than the spirit of Rome itself. Second, the last days of the Republic had not been happy for Asia Minor. Asia was the richest of all the provinces, and Asia had suffered most of all from the rapacity of avaricious Roman officials, who were willing to stoop to any crime to enrich themselves quickly in their short tenure of office. Augustus changed all that. 'Augustus had been a savior to the Asian peoples, and they deified him as "the Savior of mankind", and worshipped him with the most whole-hearted devotion as the God incarnate in human form, the "present deity". He alone stood between them and death or a life of misery and torture. They hailed the birthday of Augustus as the beginning of a new year, and worshipped the incarnate God in public and in private' (W. M. Ramsay, *The Letters to the Seven Churches*, 114, 115). The worship of Rome began in gratitude; and it was another wave of gratitude which turned it into the worship of the Emperor. H. B. Swete (*The Apocalypse of St. John*, p. lxxxv) quotes from an inscription which describes Octavian as 'the benefactor of the race of men, who has not only fulfilled our greatest hopes, but has even surpassed them, for the land and the sea are safe, and cities flourish in peace, in concord, and in prosperity'. The result of this was that the first temple was erected to the godhead of Caesar in 29 B.C. at Pergamum (Tacitus, *Annals*, iv. 37). From that time on in Asia cities struggled for the right to erect temples to the Emperor's godhead, and to gain the honorable title *neōkoros*, which means 'temple-sweeper', of such a temple. Before the end of the first century A.D. of the cities mentioned in the Revelation Smyrna, Ephesus, Pergamum, Sardis, Philadelphia, Laodicea all possessed such temples.

(*c*) The attitudes of the early emperors

But we have to go on to ask, how did this Caesar-worship become the deadly enemy of the Church, and the greatest threat to the Christian? This did not happen all at once. It is quite clear that the early Emperors were embarrassed by this worship. So far from encouraging it, they discouraged it. Augustus forbade it in Italy, and forbade it for citizens. It might be suitable for excitable Levantines, but it was entirely out of place for sober Roman citizens. Tiberius followed the example of Augustus. 'He forbade the voting of temples, flamens and priests in his honor, and even the setting up of statues and busts without his permission; and this he gave only with the understanding that they were not to be placed among the likenesses of the gods, but among the adornments of the temples' (Suetonius, *Tiberius*, 26). Once, when he was called 'Lord' (*dominus*) he rebuked the speaker for using insulting language, and when another spoke of his 'sacred duties' he substituted the word 'laborious' (Suetonius, *Tiberius*, 27). Tacitus says that Tiberius had a strong contempt for honors. He describes how he did allow Pergamum to erect a temple in his honor, simply because Augustus had already done so, but he goes on to tell how Tiberius flatly refused to allow an application from Further Spain to erect a temple to him. Tacitus puts a lengthy speech into his mouth in which he says that 'it would be a vain and arrogant thing to receive the sacred honor of images representing the divine throughout all the provinces.' 'I am mortal', he said, 'and limited to the functions of humanity' (Tacitus, *Annals*, iv. 37, 38).

(*d*) Caligula

The situation altered with Caligula, but the alteration was abnormal, because Caligula was an epileptic and a madman. Suetonius begins his account of Caligula's claims savagely: 'So much for Caligula as an emperor; we must now tell of his career as a monster'. He ordered that the statues of the gods should be brought from Greece, their heads removed, and his head put in their place. He made the temple of Castor and Pollux the vestibule of his palace and took his place between them. He erected a temple to his own godhead, complete with a priesthood, and in it a life-size statue of himself in solid gold. He talked confidently to Jupiter Capitolinus and built a bridge from his house to the Capitol. He invited the moon to his embraces and to his bed; and he executed those who were not prepared to swear by his godhead (Suetonius, *Gaius Caligula*, 22, 27). He very nearly precipitated a most dangerous situation by insisting that his image should be erected in the Holy of Holies in Jerusalem (Josephus, *Antiquities of the Jews*, xvii. 7 and 8). An army was collected to enforce this order, but fortunately he died before the storm could burst. Amongst the early Emperors Caligula stands alone in demanding worship as a god.

(*e*) Claudius

Claudius, who succeeded Caligula, was far from being a reputable character, but he had none of Caligula's desire for deification. It is true that a temple was erected to him in Ephesus, and another in Camulodunum in Britain. It was this temple which produced Boadicea's revolt, for the people of Britain regarded it as 'a citadel of perpetual tyranny', and its priesthood financially ruined those who were compelled to undertake it (Tacitus, *Annals*, xiv. 31). But on his accession the people of Alexandria sought permission to erect a temple to him and to organize a priesthood and he replied: 'I deprecate the appointment of a high priest to me, and the erection of temples, for I do not wish to be offensive to my contemporaries, and I hold that sacred fanes and the like have by all ages been attributed to the immortal gods as peculiar honors' (P. Lond, 1912; A. S. Hunt and G. C. Edgar, *Select Papyri*, ii. 80, 81).

(f) Nero

Nor did Nero, the next Emperor, take his divinity seriously, nor desire it. He was more eager to be greeted for his triumphs and for his victories as a flute-player, an actor and a charioteer, and to hear the people, as Dion Cassius tells, acclaim him on his return from Greece with eighteen hundred artistic victories to his credit with the shouts: 'Victories Olympic! Victories Pythian! Nero the Hercules! Nero Apollo! Sacred One!' Tacitus tells that Cerualis Anicius, the consul-elect, proposed that a public temple should be built to the divine Nero, implying that he 'had transcended all mortal grandeur and deserved the adoration of mankind', but this was interpreted as more likely to bring death 'seeing that divine honors are not paid to an Emperor until he has ceased to live among men' (Tacitus, *Annals*, xv. 74). It might have been expected that Nero would have claimed divine honors, but he shrank, perhaps superstitiously, from them. The Flavian Emperors, Titus and Vespasian, also accepted Caesar-worship as it was, but did nothing at all to develop, or to demand it.

Then with Domitian there came the sudden and the violent change. As we have seen, Tiberius refused to be addressed as 'Lord' (Suetonius, *Tiberius*, 27). Augustus before him had made the same refusal. Once, when he was present in the theater, the play contained the words,

> 'O just and gracious Lord!'

At the words all the people sprang to their feet and applauded, as if the words had been addressed directly to Augustus. Both by look and gesture he silenced them, and on the next day rebuked them in an edict (Suetonius, *Augustus*, 53). With Domitian it was very different. When he was reconciled to his divorced wife, he said that he had recalled her 'to the divine couch', using a word which was the technical word for the couch of the gods. When he entered the theater, he delighted to hear the people cry, 'Good fortune attend our Lord and his lady!' He began a circular letter: 'Our Lord and God (*dominus et deus noster*) bids this be done'. From then onwards this was the only way in which he might be addressed either in speech or in writing (Suetonius, *Domitian*, 13). Here we are on the verge of Caesar-worship, not tolerated, but demanded. And here we are at the time of the Revelation.

'The Keystone of Imperial Policy'

We have now seen how Caesar-worship grew from a spontaneous emergence to an imperial demand. But there was still a further step to take. The Roman Empire was vast and heterogeneous, extending as it did from Britain to the Euphrates and from the Danube to North Africa. Some kind of unifying principle was a necessity. The great unifying principle is a common religion. None of the local cults had it in it to become universal, *but Caesar-worship had*. So in the end Caesar-worship became what Mommsen called 'the keystone of imperial policy'. It became the means of unifying the Empire. Once a year all men had to come to the temple of Caesar to burn their pinch of incense, and to say: 'Caesar is Lord'. We have to note two things. First, this was obviously far more a matter of political loyalty than of religious devotion. It was an act whereby a man declared his allegiance to Caesar and to Rome. Second, it remains true that Rome was characteristically tolerant. Caesar-worship was never meant to be exclusive; once a man had affirmed his loyalty to Caesar and to the godhead of Caesar, he could go and worship any god he liked, so long as the worship did not conflict with public order and public decency.

Having paid his respects to the godhead of Caesar, a man received a certification that he had done so. One from A.D. 250 runs: 'To the commissioners of sacrifices from Aurelia Demos, without patronymic, daughter of Helena and Wife of Aurelius Irenaeus, of the quarter of the Hellenium. I have always been wont to sacrifice to the gods, and now also in your presence, in accordance with the command, I have made sacrifice and libation and tasted the offering, and I request you to certify my statement. Farewell. (Signed) I, Aurelia Demos, have presented this declaration. I, Aurelius Irenaeus wrote for her, as she is illiterate. (Attested), Aurelius Sabinus, prytanis, saw you sacrificing. (Dated) The first year of the Emperor Caesar Gaius Messius Quintus Trajanus Decius Pius Felix Augustus, Pauni 20' (P. Ryl. 12; A. S. Hunt and G. S. Edgar, *Select Papyri*, ii. [No. 319, Loeb Classical Library]).

Here, then, was the situation which was threatening the Christian, even if in the time of Revelation it had not yet completely emerged. No Christian would ever take the name 'Lord' and give it to any one other than Jesus Christ; no Christian would ever compromise by first sacrificing to the godhead of Caesar, and then going away and being a Christian. Therefore, the simple fact was that every Christian was automatically regarded as a disaffected citizen and a criminal worthy of death. The choice was quite simple – Caesar or Christ? In Sir William Watson's lines:

> So to the wild wolf Hate were sacrificed
> The panting, huddled flock, whose crime was Christ.

The Church and the Empire were over against each other – and none had ever withstood the might of Rome. Here is the situation against which the Revelation was written, and here is the particular background of its thirteenth chapter. So, then, we approach this chapter always reading it in the light of the fact that for John of the Revelation the Roman Empire is the embodiment of satanic power and Caesar-worship is the wickedness in which that satanic power finds its peak.

The Beast

The beast arises from the sea; that is to say, for some one in Asia Minor the beast comes from the West, that is, from Rome, just as the eagle does in 4 Ezra 11.1. The beast has seven heads and ten horns. The heads and the horns stand for power. The seven heads of the beast are said in 17.9 to be the seven hills on which the evil woman sits, that is, the seven hills of Rome. But it is quite clear that in this passage the heads stand for persons. They stand for the seven deified Emperors of Rome. There is nothing impossible or even difficult in the fact that the seven heads stand both for Rome and for the Emperors of Rome, for Rome was incarnated in her Emperors. The seven Emperors for whom the seven heads stand are Tiberius, Caligula, Claudius, Nero, Titus, Vespasian, and Domitian. The ten horns are more difficult. There are three main possibilities. (*a*) R. H. Charles thinks that John is working, not with material which he, so to speak, invented, but with ancient mythological material. It, therefore, sometimes happens that not all the details of John's ancient material fit into John's picture. Charles, therefore, thinks that the ten horns are no more than an archaic survival from the material which John took over, and that it is unnecessary, and indeed impossible, to attach any symbolic meaning to them. (*b*) It is just possible that the ten horns have to do with the ten main provinces of the Roman Empire – Italy, Achaea, Asia, Syria, Egypt, Africa, Spain, Gaul, Britain, Germany. The horns would then be the governors of these provinces, who exercised the imperial power, and who exercised it to impose Caesar-worship on the people. (*c*) Perhaps the third explanation is the most likely. In the list of seven Emperors as we have given it there are

in fact three names missing. After the death of Nero there came
a time of chaos during which there were three Emperors in little
more than eighteen months – Galba, Otho and Vitellius. These
Emperors cannot really be said to be heads, but they can be said
to be horns, because for their brief space they did exercise the
power of Rome. It is at least true that the beast symbolizes
Rome, and the seven heads and the ten horns stand for those
who exercised the imperial power. This is the more certain in
that on the heads there were *diadēmata*, that is *royal crowns*,
not *stephanoi*, which would be *victors' crowns*. The horns bear
the symbol of imperial majesty.

On the heads there were names – the plural is the better
reading – of blasphemy. There is no difficulty in finding imperial
titles, which would seem to the Christians names of blasphemy.
The standard name was of course *sebastos* or Augustus, which
means *reverend, to be worshipped*, an adjective which belongs to
God by right and which it would be blasphemous for any
human being to annex to himself. Frequently in edicts the later
Emperors' names are preceded by the word *theos* or *divus*,
deified. Here, indeed, was a name which was an insult to God.
Often the Emperors were addressed by the title *sōtēr*, Savior;
and a Christian would look with a shudder of horror at any man
taking to himself the title which was the title of Jesus Christ. But
it may be that John is thinking in particular of one word. The
commonest of all titles for the Emperor was *kurios, dominus,
lord*. That became the automatic title of the Emperor. 'Caesar is
Lord' may well be said to be the creed of the Roman Empire;
'Jesus Christ is Lord' may well be said to be the creed of the
Church. The application of the word *kurios* to any human being
would be the supreme blasphemy since for the Christian it was
the name of Jesus, and for the Jew it was the word in the LXX
by which the sacred name was translated into Greek.

The beast was like a leopard with a bear's feet and a lion's mouth. Here John's picture goes back to Daniel 7.3-7 in which the world empires are described in terms of beasts, for there was no other way in which to describe them. Babylonia, Media, Persia, Greece are so described. The interesting and significant fact is that the beast in the Revelation is a kind of composite figure made up of all the beasts in Daniel. The point is that the Roman Empire for John includes in itself the sum total of all wickedness that has ever been and ever can be. The dragon is Satan, the Devil (12.8-9), and to the beast the devil has given his power and his authority. That is to say Satan exercises his power through the satanic wickedness of the Roman Empire and in particular through Caesar-worship. Here is a principle which is eternally valid, and which is eternally a warning. God is ever looking for men to use, and so is Satan. Just as God is seeking for hands to do His work, so is Satan. Good seeks to express itself in the world, and so does evil, and both can only express themselves through persons. Both men and nations have the choice of allowing themselves to be used by God or the devil.

Nero Resurrected

One of the heads had the appearance of having been dead, and of being restored to life again. Here is a picture of a kind of diabolical resurrection, and it comes from an idea which haunted Rome for many a day; it comes from the *Nero Redivivus*, the Nero Resurrected legend. Such was the joy of the people that they danced in the streets when Nero died (Suetonius, *Nero*, 57). It may be that there was a kind of vague idea that Nero was so wicked as to be immortal in his wickedness. There was a belief that he was not dead. There were some who still read out his edicts, as if he was still alive, and would come back to deal death and destruction to his enemies. It was indeed said that during his life-time astrologers had told Nero that he would lose his throne, but would find another in the East, some said in Jerusalem, some in Parthia (Suetonius, *Nero*, 40). As early as A.D. 69 a pretender emerged to claim that he was Nero (Tacitus, *History*, ii. 8, 9). He was variously described as a slave from Pontus or a freedman from Italy. He was, like Nero, a skilful harp-player and he bore a certain resemblance to him. He gained a following among those whom Tacitus called 'deserters and needy vagrants'; he even seduced some soldiers from their loyalty. Achaea and Asia Minor were in a highly explosive condition. The adventurer took to sea, but was pursued by Galba's emissary Calpurnius Asprenas, and was finally killed. In A.D. 80 another pretender arose; and finally in A.D. 88 still another pretender arose, this time in Parthia, and came within an ace of launching the armies of Parthia against Rome (Tacitus, *History*, i. 2; Suetonius, *Nero*, 51). The prevalence of this *Nero Redivivus* legend is shown by its prominence in the *Sibylline Oracles*. His imagined flight to the East is described: 'Then shall flee from Babylon [that is, Rome] a kind fearful and shameless whom all mortals and all the best men loathe. For he destroyed many and laid his hands on the womb [that is, murdered his mother] and sinned against wives and was born of abominable parentage. He shall come to the Medes and the kings of the Persians, . . . making his lair with these evil men against the true people' (v. 143-149). His return is pictured: 'There shall come from the ends of the earth a matricide fleeing and devising sharp-edged plans in his mind. He shall ruin all the earth, and gain all power, . . . And he shall destroy many men and great tyrants, and shall burn all men as none ever did' (v. 363-369). 'To the west shall come the strife of gathering war, and the exile from Rome, brandishing a mighty sword, crossing the Euphrates with many myriads' (iv. 137-139).

In the popular mythology of the latter half of the first century there was deeply embedded this picture of the returning Nero, *Nero Redivivus*, Nero Resurrected. At least in some spheres of Christian thought *Nero Redivivus* and Antichrist coalesced. The coming Antichrist was thought of in terms of *Nero Redivivus*.

That is the picture of our chapter. There is a kind of climax of evil. The Roman Empire is the instrument of Satan, the earthly body through which Satan exercises his power. That evil is centered in Caesar-worship which took the name Lord from Christ and gave it to Caesar, and which tried to coerce all men into doing likewise. And this evil power will find its most terrible manifestation in the return to life of the head that was wounded to death, in the coming of Nero-Antichrist, who would try with still more power and cruelty to impose this evil worship upon men and to dethrone God and Jesus Christ.

The Forty-two Months

In *v*. 5 we read that the power which was given to the Beast which came from the sea was to last *forty and two months*. This is a figure which occurs in the Revelation in more than one form. It occurs in the same form as here in 11.2; in 12.6 it occurs in the form of a thousand two hundred and threescore days; and in 12.14 it occurs in the form of a time, and times and half a time. The last of these phrases is from Daniel 7.25 and it is common in apocalyptic imagery. It is the common extent of a period of limited but intense suffering. Its origin comes from the sorest time of terror which ever descended on the Jewish nation. In the first half of the second century B.C. Antiochus Epiphanes made a quite deliberate attempt to wipe out Jewish religion. He was a lover of all things Greek, and he considered himself an apostle of Greek culture. It was further the fact that Israel lay precisely between his own kingdom of Syria and that of his deadly and bitter rival Egypt, and the subjugation of Israel would naturally have aided his designs against Egypt. Antiochus Epiphanes descended on Israel. There followed a time when even to possess a copy of the Law, and even to circumcise a child, was a crime punishable by death. The Temple was desecrated, the priests' chambers were turned into public brothels, the great altar of the burnt-offering was turned into an altar to Zeus, and the Temple courts were defiled by the offering of swine's flesh and the pouring out on them of swine's blood. History has seldom seen such a deliberate attempt to obliterate a nation's faith. It was then that Judas Maccabaeus and the rest of his heroic family arose; and after a bitter struggle against incredible odds the Jews regained their liberty. The point of this apocalyptic reference is that the desecration of the Temple lasted from June 168 B.C. to December 165 B.C. The restoration and the purification of the Temple is still celebrated by the Jews in the Feast of Hanukah, which falls at the same time as the Christian Christmas. This is to say that never-to-be forgotten desecration of the Temple lasted for almost exactly three and a half years. Forty-two months and a thousand two hundred and threescore days are the same as three and a half years. A time, times and half a time means a year, two years and half a year, once again giving the period three and a half years. The time of desecration during the invasion of Antiochus Epiphanes had so burned itself into the minds and memories of the Jewish nation that it came to be used regularly to denote the period of terror, under the sway of demonic evil, before the final ending of history came.

Verse 10 is a curious verse. The meaning is that in the time of intense terror and evil which is coming human resistance is of no avail. The world is beyond cure, it is in the ineluctable grip of evil; at such a time nothing but steadfast endurance can avail. The struggle is not a human struggle; it is a struggle between God and the devil; and those who have to go through it can only endure until the end comes, and their vindication follows. Human participation in this struggle consists only in waiting upon God.

The Beast from the Land

In *v.* 11 another beast emerges, this time a beast from the land. It is said of this beast from the land that it exercises all the power of the first beast, which came from the sea, and that it causes men to worship the first beast. We have seen that the first beast represents the power of Rome, and in particular the Caesar-worship which that power propagated and on which it insisted. This Caesar-worship was highly organized in each province. It was organized into communes or presbyteries or dioceses, with priests and officials and a powerful and effective administration. The beast from the land represents the provincial organization for the spread and the enforcement of Caesar-worship. The beast from the land is the complement, the agent, the instrument of the beast from the sea, and it represents the local organization through which Caesar-worship operated within the province.

The Image of the Beast

Verses 14-16 speak about the image of the beast, and about wonders connected with it. The expression of devotion to the image of the Emperor was something which was well known. Tacitus tells of the ceremony, when Corbulo had defeated Tiridates, and had thus avenged the surrender of the Roman legions. 'It was then arranged that Tiridates should place the ensign of royalty beneath the image of Caesar, and only receive it again from the hand of Nero. . . . A few days afterwards there was a grand review of the two armies. On one side were the Parthian cavalry, drawn up in their squadrons, and under their national ensigns; on the other stood the Roman legions, with their eagles and standards glistening and with the images of their gods set up as in a temple. Between the two armies was a tribunal, supporting a curule chair; and on the chair was the effigy of Nero. The customary sacrifices having been offered,

Tiridates advanced, took the diadem off his head, and laid it at the feet of the effigy' (Tacitus, *Annals*, xv. 29 [G. G. Ramsay's translation]). Here we have an example of the image of the Emperor literally standing for the Emperor, and of a fallen foe doing obeisance to the image.

This is precisely the kind of thing which our verses imply. As for the wonders connected with the image – the fire, the miracles, the apparent life, the speaking voice – the priests of the ancient cults were skilled in producing life-like effects by the use of ventriloquism and mechanical apparatus and all kinds of jugglery. The provincial Caesar-worship organization would have no difficulty in seeing to it that the imperial images produced startling and life-like effects.

The Mark of the Beast

Verse 16 goes on to tell how those who accept and worship and submit to the beast receive a mark on their right hand, or on their forehead. The idea of some kind of mark, as in some sense indicating ownership or allegiance, was very common in the ancient world.

Slaves were sometimes branded with a mark of ownership. This was specially so if the slave had been a runaway, for in that case he was branded on the forehead with the letters FUG which stand for *fugitivus*, which means *runaway*. So often did this happen that slaves were sometimes with a grim punning jest called *literati, the lettered ones*. History has one grim example of the branding of captives. After their disastrous defeat under Nicias in the Sicilian campaign certain of the Athenians who were taken captive were branded on the forehead with the sign of a galloping horse, which was the Sicilian emblem (Plutarch, *Nicias*, 29). The sign of ownership and subjection was branded on them. Ambrose says of slaves that they were 'inscribed with the seal of their master' (*De Obit. Valentin.*, 58).

There is some evidence that soldiers were branded on the hand with the name of their general. These marks are generally called *stigmata*. Aelian says that soldiers bear their *stigmata* on their hands: and Ambrose goes on to say that soldiers are signed with the name of their general. It has been suggested that this was in Paul's mind when he said that he bore in his body the *stigmata* of Christ (Galatians 6.17), and that he may have been calling himself thereby the *miles Christi*, the soldier of Christ.

There is definite evidence that devotees of gods were branded with the symbol of the god whom they worshipped. The account in 3 Maccabees tells how Ptolemy IV Philopator decreed that 'all Jews should be degraded to the lowest rank, and to the condition of slaves; and that those who spoke against it should be taken by force and put to death; and that these when they were registered should be marked with a brand on their bodies with the ivy-leaf, the emblem of Bacchus' (3 Maccabees 2.28, 29).

To bear the mark of a person would mean either that one belonged to that person, as a slave or a soldier, or that one was devoted to that person, as the worshipper of a god.

In the Old Testament we read of sacred marking. The Jews are forbidden to cut themselves, and this seems to be prohibition of sacred protective marking, which distinguished people as being under the protection of some god (Leviticus 19.28, 21.5, Deuteronomy 14.1). Cain has a mark put upon him in order that he may not be slain (Genesis 4.15). In Ezekiel the faithful are marked upon the forehead before the avenging wrath is let loose (Ezekiel 9.1-4). Thus the mark would mean that the person was under the protection of the god. In our present passage of the Revelation this mark of the beast may be a grim and blasphemous parody of the protective sealing of the faithful in 7.1-3. Just as God has those who bear his mark so Satan has those who bear his.

Before we leave this conception of the mark, we may cite two further things which shed light on it. Deissmann has pointed out (*Light from the Ancient East*, 344f.) that it was the custom to impress on deeds of sale and similar documents a stamp containing the name of the Emperor and the year of his reign; that stamp is actually called a *charagma*, which is the very word the Revelation here uses. This would mean that those who bear the mark of the beast have the seal of their Satanic Emperor upon them. Such imperial stamps have been found dating back to A.D. 48.

There is one curious third or fourth century papyrus letter (*P. Oxy.* 1680) from a son to his father Apollo. Father and son are for the time being separated, times are dangerous and unsettled, and the son fears that something may happen to the father. He writes: 'Dearest father, I pray to the god for your prosperity and success and that we may receive you home in good health. I have indeed told you before of my grief at your absence from among us, and my fear that something dreadful might happen to you and that we may not find your body. Indeed I often wish to tell you that having regard to the insecurity I wanted *to stamp a mark* upon you.' The verb used is *encharaxai*, the verb with which *charagma* is connected. Here the idea is clearly that of an identifying mark – perhaps a tattoo mark – by which the body may be known. Even so, those who belong to the beast are marked with a mark which identifies them as his.

Verse 17 declares that in the time of terror things would be ordered in such a way that only those who had the mark of the beast would be able to engage in the ordinary business and affairs of life. It was not indeed to be long before the Christian found many a trade or profession either impossible for him or barred to him. Later Tertullian in his *On Idolatry* was to deal with this very problem. Any craftsman – the mason, the builder, the carpenter, the tailor, the woodcarver, the metalworker, the scribe – might suddenly find himself involved in work connected with a heathen temple or with heathen worship. Many such workers asked how they could possibly give up their work and still make a living. But Tertullian insists that the Lord's sayings are 'examples which take away all excuse'. 'What is it that you say? "I shall be in need". But the Lord calls the needy "happy". "I shall have no food". But "think not", says he, "about food". And as for an example of clothing, we have the lilies. "My work was my subsistence". Nay, but, "all things are to be sold, and divided to the needy". "But provision must be made for children and posterity". "None putting his hand on the plow, and looking back is fit for work." "But I was under contract." "No one can serve two masters." . . . Parents, wives, children have to be left behind for God's sake.' The problem of the Christian's exclusion from the business and social life of the community was to be very real.

At that stage it was still a voluntary exclusion; it was a case of the Christian demonstrating, as Tertullian put it, that 'faith does not fear famine'. But the time was to come when the exclusion was to be much more radical. Early in A.D. 250 Decius issued his edict against Christianity. Provincial governors and magistrates, assisted by local committees of prominent citizens, were to see to it that on a certain fixed day all men sacrificed to the gods and to the genius of the Emperor, and tasted the sacrifices. Thereafter they would receive a certificate that they had done so. Such a certificate runs: 'To the superintendents of offerings and sacrifices at the city from Aurelius . . . thion son of Theodorus and Pantonymis, of the said city. It has ever been my custom to make sacrifices and libations to the gods, and now also in your presence I have in accordance with the command poured libations and sacrificed and tasted the offerings together with my son Aurelius Dioscurus and my daughter Aurelia Lais. I therefore request you to certify my statement. The first year of the Emperor Caesar Gaius Messius Quintus Trajanus Decius

Pius Felix Augustus, Pauni 20' (*P. Oxy.* 658: other examples in
H. B. Workman, *Persecution in the Early Church*, 341; and in *A.
S. Hunt and G. C. Edgar, Select Papyri*, ii. 352-355). The time
was to come when, unless a man possessed that certificate, he
was cut off from all ordinary life, and faced with imprisonment,
banishment and death. Such a certificate in the time to come
might well seem the mark of the beast.

The Number of the Beast

Finally, we come to the most fascinating problem in this chapter
of problems. In *v.* 18 we are told that the number of the beast
is 666; it is to be noted that there is an alternative reading 616;
but the first reading is certainly correct. This is to say, that the
person who is the apotheosis of evil is concealed in the number
666. Here we come on a phenomenon called *isopsēphia*. The
basis of this *isopsēphia* is in the fact that Greek has no numerals,
and that the letters of the alphabet each have a numerical value.
Therefore, any series of letters may form a word and may also
form a number. This *isopsēphia* had many manifestations. To
begin with the very simplest of them, there exists a scribbled
piece of writing on the walls of Pompeii: 'I love her whose
number is 545' (A. Deissmann, *ib.*, 276). The lover identifies –
and conceals – his love by adding up the numerical value of the
letters in her name! When the John of the Revelation
symbolized the beast under a number, he was using a method
with which even scribblers on walls were perfectly familiar.

It must be noted here and now at the beginning that this
custom existed not only among the Greeks but also among the
Hebrews in the form of *gematria*. To take an example the
Hebrew word *nāḥāṣ*, which means *serpent* has the same
numerical value as the Hebrew word *māṣiaḥ* which means
Messiah; it was thus argued that *serpent* is one of the titles of the
Messiah; and it is further suggested that this may have some

relation to the fact that the New Testament says that Moses lifted up the *serpent* in the wilderness (John 3.14). So to the Jews also this method of identification and concealment was perfectly familiar.

Isopsēphia was not infrequently used in matters of religion. The god Thouth was known by the number 1218, because that is the numerical value of his name; *th* = 9; *ō* = 800; *u* = 400; *th* = 9: Total 1218. Jupiter or Zeus was known as 717, because one of his titles is *hē archē* and 717 is the numerical value of that phrase – *ē* = 8; *a* = 1; *r* = 100; *ch* = 600; *ē* = 8: Total 717. One of the commonest words on amulets is *abrasax* or *abraxas*. The reason is that the sum of these letters is 365 – a = 1; *b* = 2; *r* = 100; *a* = 1; *x* = 60; *a* = 1; *s* = 200: Total 365. And 365 is both the total of the days of the year and the number of the heavens and the value of the name Meithras (Mithras) – *M* = 40; *e* = 5; *i* = 10; *th* = 9; *r* = 100; *a* = 1; *s* = 200: Total 365.

One of the most interesting appearances of this practice was in the days of Nero. People wrote on the walls what they were afraid to say of him, and passed round jests and criticisms of him. One of these is retailed by Suetonius (*Nero*, 39). It runs:

A calculation new. Nero his mother slew.

This was written in Greek, and the point is that the numerical value of the letters in *Nero* is the same as the numerical value of the letters in the rest of the sentence. Therefore, Nero = the slayer of one's own mother, and when the Romans wrote this on the walls they were accusing Nero of being a matricide.

This even got into Christian exegesis. The Epistle of Barnabas (ix. 7, 8) takes Genesis 14.14 where Abraham is said to have won the victory with three hundred and eighteen of his household. Eighteen in Greek is *iē*, which are the first two letters of Jesus's name; three hundred is *t*, which is the Cross;

therefore, this is a prefiguring of the victory of the Cross. Tertullian found Gideon's three hundred another prefiguring of the Cross (*Carm. adv. Marc.*, iii. 4). The fascination of numbers laid hold even on the early exegetes.

Before we proceed to the more elaborate solutions, there are certain simpler ones that we may clear away. There are some few who have wished to take the number 666 chronologically. In A.D. 1213 Pope Innocent III called for a new crusade because he held that Muhammadan power was destined to last for six hundred and sixty-six years, and at that time that period was near to an end. Certain others have taken it to refer to the six hundred and sixty-six years between Seleucus in 311 B.C. and the emergence of Julian the Apostate in A.D. 355. Finally, it has been suggested that the reference is to the year A.D. 666, in which year, it is said, Pope Vitalian decreed that all public worship should be in Latin. It is so clear that the number stands for a name that these suggestions can at once be disregarded.

Six hundred and sixty-six has been connected with the numerical value of the name *Jesus*; the letters of Jesus give the number 888 – $i = 10$; $\bar{e} = 8$; $s = 200$; $o = 70$; $u = 400$; $s = 200$: Total 888. It is said that 777 would stand for perfection; that 888 will, therefore, stand for more than perfection, which is in Jesus, and that 666 will stand for imperfection, which is in Antichrist.

We now come to the names which this number has been taken to represent, and for this we are indebted to the great store of information in the old commentaries of A. E. Elliott and Moses Stuart.

Three names were suggested by Irenaeus. (1) *Euanthas*: $E = 5$; $u = 400$; $a = 1$; $n = 50$; $th = 9$; $a = 1$; $s = 200$: Total 666. But the word Euanthas is itself meaningless. (2) *Teitan*: $T = 300$; $e = 5$; $i = 10$; $t = 300$; $a = 1$; $n = 50$. This could be taken as a reference to the Titans who rebelled against the gods, or it could be used as a reference to the Emperor Titus, who was not however a persecutor. (3) *Lateinos*: $L = 30$; $a = 1$; $t = 300$; $e = 5$; $i = 10$; $n = 50$; $o = 70$; $s = 200$: Total 666. This is a popular solution. It could stand for the Roman Empire, and it can be made also to stand for the Roman Church.

Primasius suggested the word *arnoume*: $a = 1$; $r = 100$; $n = 50$; $o = 70$; $u = 400$; $m = 40$; $e = 5$: Total 666. The word *arnoume* itself is meaningless, but it could be connected with the verb *arneisthai*, to deny, and so mean apostate.

Arethas suggested several solutions. (1) *ho nikētēs*: $o = 70$; $n = 50$; $i = 10$; $k = 20$; $ē = 8$; $t = 300$; $ē = 8$; $s = 200$: Total 666. (2) *kakos hodēgos*: $k = 20$; $a = 1$; $k = 20$; $o = 70$; $s = 200$; $o = 70$; $d = 4$; $ē = 8$; $g = 3$; $o = 70$; $s = 200$: Total 666. This would mean *the evil leader*. (3) *amnos adikos*: $a = 1$; $m = 40$; $n = 50$; $o = 70$; $s = 200$; $a = 1$; $d = 4$; $i = 10$; $k = 20$; $o = 70$; $s = 200$: Total 666. This would mean *the evil lamb*.

The interesting and significant thing about all this is that it is proof that the meaning of the number was just as mysterious in the Early Church as it is today.

We now come to modern interpretations. The number is a favorite playground of those who wish to find Antichrist in the Roman Catholic Church. The following solutions have been offered. (1) *Italika ekklēsia*: $i = 10$; $t = 300$; $a = 1$; $l = 30$; $i = 10$; $k = 20$; $a = 1$; $e = 5$; $k = 20$; $k = 20$; $l = 30$; $ē = 8$; $s = 200$; $i = 10$; $a = 1$: Total 666. Elliott remarks that the name of no other national Church will give the same result! (2) *hē Latinē basileia*: $ē = 8$; $L = 30$; $a = 1$; $t = 300$; $i = 10$; $n = 50$; $ē = 8$; $b = 2$; $a = 1$; $s = 200$; $i = 10$; $l = 30$; $e = 5$; $i = 10$; $a = 1$: Total 666. Mr. Clarke who discovered this solution says that he tried it out on more than four hundred other kingdoms without again getting the result 666! (3) *Papeiskos*: $P = 80$; $a = 1$; $p = 80$; $e = 5$; $i = 10$; $s = 200$; $k = 20$; $o = 70$; $s = 200$: Total 666. *Papeiskos* is of course taken to mean Pope.

As is only to be expected Roman Catholic attempts have been made to turn the tables, and the following two solutions may be quoted. (1) *Loutherana*: L = 30; o = 70; u = 400; th = 9; e = 5; r = 100; a = 1; n = 50; a = 1: Total 666. This, of course, is an alleged form of the name Luther. (2) *Saxoneios*: S = 200; a = 1; x = 60; o = 70; n = 50; e = 5; i = 10; o = 70; s = 200: Total 666. This is alleged to mean the Saxon, and is again intended to represent Luther.

Finally, in the realm of fantasy, we may look at certain of the interpretations which have seen certain great figures in this number. (1) *Maometis*: M = 40; a = 1; o = 70; m = 40; e = 5; t = 300; i = 10; s = 200: Total 666. This, of course, is a reference to Muhammad. (2) *Na Bonapartia*: N = 50; a = 1; B = 2; o = 70; n = 50; a = 1; p = 80; a = 1; r = 100; t = 300; i = 10; a = 1: Total 666. This is a reference to Napoleon! (3) If A = 100, B = 101, C = 102 and so on, the following result can be obtained: H = 107; I = 108; T = 119; L = 111; E = 104; R = 117: HITLER = 666!

We may briefly note that some people have sought solutions in Latin. The difficulty here is that not all Latin letters have numerical equivalents; and therefore only the letters with equivalents can be counted. We may cite two of these 'solutions'. (1) The title of the Pope – VICARIUS GENERALIS DEI IN TERRIS; V = 5; I = 1; C = 100; I = 1; V = 5; L = 50; I = 1; D = 500; I = 1; I = 1; I = 1: Total 666. (2) One of the great persecuting Emperors Diocletian named thus – DIOCLES AUGUSTUS; D = 500; I = 1; C = 100; L = 50; V = 5; V = 5; V = 5: Total 666.

Moses Stuart, having dealt with what he considers fantastic solutions, says: '*Pudet has nugas!*' (One is ashamed of such nonsense). Even so, let us turn finally to the solutions which may be right. (1) Caligula was the Roman Emperor who actually tried to put his own image in the Holy of Holies. His name was in Greek *Gaios Kaisar*: $G = 3$; $a = 1$; $i = 10$; $o = 70$; $s = 200$; $K = 20$; $a = 1$; $i = 10$; $s = 200$; $a = 1$; $r = 200$: Total 616. This would be a good solution but it gives us the inferior alternative reading of 616. (2) Deissmann favored the solution *Kaisar Theos*: $K = 20$; $a = 1$; $i = 10$; $s = 200$; $a = 1$; $r = 100$; $Th = 9$; $e = 5$; $o = 70$; $s = 200$. This would be in many ways the best solution of all, but again it results in the number of the inferior reading.

We are in the end left, we think, with only one possible solution. And it is a solution which works in Hebrew and not in Greek letters. This is in fact doubly likely. It is clear that the John of the Revelation thought in Hebrew, if he did not actually first write in Hebrew; and, if the number represents a Hebrew name the disguise is doubly impenetrable. We think the solution is almost certainly *NRWN QSR*; Neron Caesar; $N = 50$; $R = 200$; $W = 6$; $N = 50$; $Q = 100$; $S = 60$; $R = 200$: Total 666; and, if the final N in Nero is dropped to bring the word into line with its Latin form the result is 616, which would explain the alternative reading.

The writer of the Revelation saw in the Roman Empire and its Emperor worship a Satanic power; and he saw that power culminate in the return of *Nero Redivivus*, the antichrist.

6
Matthew 24:
The Mysterious Prediction

Matthew 24, with its parallels in Mark 13 and Luke 21, is a passage which has always exercised a fascination over the minds of students of the New Testament. The conservative critic would no doubt accept it entirely as the *ipsissima verba* of Jesus. Montefiore dismisses it as unauthentic and even unedifying. Scholars such as Moffatt, McNeile, Rawlinson and Branscombe see in it in one form or another a Jewish – Christian apocalypse. The commonest form of this view is to see in it a Christian document built up by Mark on the basis of a 'fly leaf' issued by some Christian prophet, speaking in the name of Jesus, in the dreadful days which preceded the last siege and the final fall of Jerusalem. Vincent Taylor sees in it a document, containing embedded in it original sayings of Jesus, which have been adapted to the doctrinal and catechetical needs of the Church at the time when Mark wrote. In a study such as this it is unnecessary to discuss these various points of view. The one thing of which we can be sure is that this chapter contains the views of the future which the Apostolic Church held, and must thus go back to what they believed that Jesus had said.

Five Strands of Teaching

There is no doubt whatever that the chapter contains sayings about different future events. The intermingling of subjects can be seen at the very beginning of the passage in the different ways in which the question of the disciples to Jesus is phrased. Jesus and his disciples were leaving the Temple courts. The disciples commented on the size and the magnificence of the stones in the building – and well they might. Josephus tells us of stones forty feet long, by twelve feet high, by eighteen feet wide, and of columns which the united arms of three men could scarcely span (Josephus, *Antiquities of the Jews*, XV. xi. 3-5). Jesus' answer was that the day would come when not one of these great stones would be left upon another, and when the whole building would be totally destroyed (Matthew 24.2, Mark 13.1, 2, Luke 21.5, 6). So far the story is related in all three Gospels in the same way. Then comes the divergence. Both Mark and Luke then go on to say that the disciples asked Jesus when these things would happen (Mark 13.4, Luke 21.7); but Matthew adds something: 'When shall these things be? and what shall be the sign of thy coming, and of the end of the world?' (Matthew 24.3). Matthew has turned an *historical* question into an *eschatological* question. This is in any event characteristic of Matthew; but it does mean that we are already warned that in what follows we are going to find two strands of material – one which deals with the historical future, and one which deals with the eschatological future.

(*a*) The Coming Destruction of Jerusalem

Let us, then, disentangle the first strand of the material, the strand which deals with the coming destruction of Jerusalem within history. We find that material in Matthew 24.15-22, Mark 13.14-20, Luke 21.20-24; (cf. Luke 19.42, 43). There is not the slightest doubt that Jesus, speaking as a prophet, foretold the destruction of Jerusalem. This material stands out with unmistakable clarity; this section clearly deals not with the Second Coming and not with the eschatological events but with the final siege and the ultimate fall of Jerusalem.

Everything that Jesus said was abundantly fulfilled. That time would begin with the abomination of desolation, the desolating sacrilege, standing in the Holy Place (Matthew 24.15, Mark 13.14; the phrase is absent from Luke). The origin of the phrase is clear, although the precise meaning of it remains in doubt. The phrase comes from Daniel (9.27, 11.31, 12.11). It describes the desecration of the Temple by Antiochus Epiphanes in 168 to 165 B.C. The writer of 1 Maccabees says: 'Now the fifteenth day of the month Casleu, in the hundred and forty-fifth year, they set up the abomination of desolation upon the altar, and builded idol altars through the cities of Juda on every side' (1 Maccabees 1.54). The erection of the altar to Olympian Zeus, the offering of swine's flesh, the complete desecration of the Temple are all included in the phrase. In the year A.D. 40 history was within an ace of repeating itself, for it was in that year that the mad Roman Emperor Caligula decided to introduce his own statue into the Holy of Holies, a blasphemous project which was halted by his death in the following year. It is not necessary to define strictly what the desolating sacrifice here is. It is certain that Jewish thought looked forward to the invasion of earth by a supramundane incarnation of evil; just as there was a divine Messiah, so there would be a devilish Messiah. Such a figure appears as the Man of Sin in II Thessalonians 2.3; as devilish symbolic figures of Rome in Revelation 17; as the antichrist in I John 4.3. It is enough to see that Jesus is saying that the terrible history of the time of Antiochus Epiphanes will repeat itself, but in an even more ultimate form, and that the incarnation and the quintessence of evil will desecrate, despoil and destroy the Temple.

At such a time they are to flee to the mountains with such haste that they do not even wait to pick up their essential baggage. That is precisely what the people did not do when the last terrible time came; they crowded into the city with consequences which were disastrous. The final siege and fall of Jerusalem form one of the most terrible stories in all history. Josephus says that ninety-seven thousand were taken captive, and eleven hundred thousand perished by the sword and by slow starvation. Josephus describes the famine of the siege: 'Then did the famine widen its progress, and devoured the people by whole houses and families; the upper rooms were full of women and children that were dying of famine; and the lanes of the cities were full of the dead bodies of the aged; the children also and the young men wandered about the marketplaces like shadows, all swelled with famine, and fell down dead wheresoever their misery seized them. As for burying them, those that were sick themselves were not able to do it; and those that were hearty and well were deterred from doing it by the great multitude of these dead bodies, and by the uncertainty there was how soon they would die themselves, for many died as they were burying others, and many went to their coffins before the fatal hour was come. Nor was there any lamentation made under these calamities, nor were heard any mournful complaints; but the famine confounded all natural passions; for those who were just going to die looked on those who were gone to their rest before them with dry eyes and open mouths. A deep silence also and a kind of deadly night had seized upon the city . . . and everyone of them died with their eyes fixed upon the Temple' (Josephus, *Wars of the Jews*, V. xii. 3). Josephus tells a dreadful story of a woman who in those days killed, roasted and ate her suckling child (*ib.*, VI. iii. 4). He tells that even the Romans, when they entered the city, were so horror-stricken by its sights, that they could not plunder it. 'When the Romans were come to the houses to plunder them, they found in them entire families of dead men, and the upper rooms full of dead corpses. . . . They then stood on a horror of this sight, and went out without touching anything' (*ib.*, VI. viii.

5). Jesus also was a prophet who warned men of the disaster to come.

They are to hope and pray that the time for flight will not be in the winter-time; it will be a time of agony for those who have little children to care for. And they are to pray that the time for flight will not come on the Sabbath (Matthew 24.20). The point of this curious phrase is this. Time and time again the Jews had suffered terribly rather than break the Sabbath Law, which forbade all activity on the Sabbath days. In the early days of the Maccabaean revolt a company of Jews who had taken refuge in caves were wiped out without lifting a hand to defend themselves because it was the Sabbath day (Josephus, *Antiquities of the Jews*, XII. vi. 2). During his siege of the city, Pompey was able to erect a mound from which to menace the defenders, because the Jewish defenders would not lift a hand to stop the builders of the mound on the Sabbath day (Josephus, *Wars of the Jews*, I. vii. 3). A rigidly orthodox Jew became helpless even to defend himself on the Sabbath day, although there was general agreement among the less extreme that even on the Sabbath day defensive action might be taken.

There is, then, in this chapter one strand of material which deals with the fall of Jerusalem. Walking in the succession of the prophets who could tell where the trends of history were moving, Jesus saw that the intransigence of the Jews could have no other end than their total destruction – and that destruction came.

(*b*) Predictions of Persecution

Before we leave the strands of this passage which deal with history within time, we may note that it also contains the prediction of persecution (Matthew 24.9). The Christians are to be delivered up to be afflicted and to be killed, and are to be universally hated for the sake of the name of Jesus. Luke and

Mark (Luke 21.12-19, Mark 13.9-13) add to this material which Matthew has in 10.17-22 which tells how the Holy Spirit will tell them what to say in the hour of need, and how even the members of the same family will turn against each other, and will betray each other.

Once again, this prophecy was abundantly fulfilled. The Christians were savagely hated. H. B. Workman (*Persecution in the Early Church*, 189, 190 footnote) collects a series of heathen verdicts on Christianity. Tacitus called it a deadly superstition (*exitiabilis superstitio*; Annals, xv. 44); Suetonius (*Nero*, 16) a new and pernicious superstition (*superstitio nova et malefica*); Pliny (*Epistles*, x. 96) a depraved and extravagant superstition (*superstitio prava et immodica*). Marcus Aurelius spoke of 'the sheer obstinacy' of the Christians (*Meditations*, ii. 3). Tertullian quotes the verdict that the Christians were 'public enemies' (*publici hostes*; *Apology*, 35). In the *Octavius* of Minucius Felix (here Workman's references require correction) Caecilius calls Christianity 'a vain and mad superstition' (*vana et demens superstitio* [ix. 3]); 'an unlawful and desperate faction' (*inlicitae ac desperatae factionis* [viii. 3]); he calls the Christian meetings 'abominable shrines of an impious assembly' (*sacraria taeterrima impiae coitionis* [ix. 1]); he declares Christianity to be 'a confederacy to be rooted out and detested' (*eruenda et execranda consensio* [ix. 1]); and he speaks of the Christians as 'a people lurking in dens and darkness' (*latebrosa et lucifuga natio* [viii. 4]).

There is no question of the hatred. The main cause of that hatred is to be seen in the other threat which hung over the Christians. They were to be hated and betrayed by even their own family. The heathen might accuse the Christians of cannibalism and immorality in the Sacrament and in the Love Feast; the Roman Government might charge the Christians with revolutionary tendencies because they would not say: 'Caesar is

Lord'; but the supreme cause of heathen hatred was in fact the effect of Christianity upon family life. 'Tampering with family relationships' (I Peter 4.15) was a charge which was early made against the Christians. There were occasions when it was bitterly true that Jesus had come to send within the family, not peace, but a sword (Matthew 10.34, 35). Justin Martyr (*Second Apology*, 2) tells of a woman who became a Christian, and who determined to reform her own life and the life of her heathen husband. The husband remained stubbornly set in his heathen ways and in his heathen morals. The woman, therefore, determined to obtain a divorce. The revenge of the husband was immediately to denounce her and her teacher Ptolemy as Christians. Literally, the wife was handed over by the husband.

By the second century the Christians themselves were not altogether blameless, and to some extent at least brought persecution upon themselves. There were those of them who took literally the injunction to call no man 'father' (Matthew 23.9). Workman points out that in Gaul at least Christian inscriptions rarely mention parentage. Lucian of Antioch was asked by the Judge of what parents he was, and he answered: 'A Christian's only relatives are the saints'. Sometimes the Christians deliberately destroyed the family ties. Further, there came an increasing and mistaken emphasis on virginity and on so-called 'chastity'. In the *Acts of Paul and Thecla* (ii) Demas describes Paul's influence: 'He deprives young men of wives and maidens of husbands by saying that in no other way shall there be a resurrection for you save by remaining chaste and keeping the flesh chaste'. In Ruinart's *Acts of the Martyrs* (27th April, 304) we read of the trial of Pollio, a reader. The Judge describes the Christians: 'You mean those people who impose on silly women and tell them that they must not marry, and persuade them to adopt a fanciful chastity'.

The day indeed came when the Christians – sometimes

inevitably, and sometimes through their own unwisdom – were hated of all men for the sake of the name of Jesus Christ.

(c) False Messiahs

There is one other strand of this chapter which falls at least partly within history. It predicts the coming of false Messiahs, pretending Christs, and deceiving teachers. This strand is to be found in Matthew 24.4, 5, 11, 12, 23-26 (cf. Mark 13.5, 6, 21, 22, Luke 17.23, 21.8, 9). Once again Jesus' prophetic insight was profoundly right. It was the coming of a false Messiah which added the last terrible touches to the destruction of Jerusalem and indeed to the desolation of the whole of Judaea in the years 132 to 135.

At that time Hadrian was Emperor. He had a passion for rebuilding and for restoration. He, therefore, planned to rebuild the shattered Jerusalem. But he did not intend to rebuild it for the Jews; it was to become Aelia Capitolina, a Roman city, with the shrines of Jupiter and Venus in it, and an edict was to be passed making circumcision illegal on the grounds that it was mutilation. Not only in Palestine, but all over the world the Jews were roused to fury. In Palestine there emerged a strange figure called Bar-Kokheba. The name means Son of the Star, and it is founded on the prophecy in Numbers 24.17. It may be that Bar-Kokheba was almost forced into his Messianic claims. The greatest Jewish Rabbi of the time was Akiba. He was so much a friend of the people that he was called 'The Hand of the Poor'. He was so great an expert in, and expounder of, the Law that he was regarded as a second Ezra. He was convinced that Bar-Kokheba was indeed the Messiah, and even became his armor-bearer. At first the rebellion was successful, for the Romans had no great military forces in Palestine, but, when Hadrian saw the conflagration which had been kindled, he recalled the great soldier Sextus Julius Severus from Britain to deal with it. There followed a war to the death, a war of extermination. The Jewish dead amounted to five hundred thousand, and as W. D. Morrison puts it (*The Jews under Roman Rule*, 203) the Jewish captives 'glutted the slave markets of the East'. Palestine was devastated with such a devastation that the effect of it remained down even to the present century. The very name Judaea was blotted out and the province became Syria Palaestina. The Jews were forbidden ever to set foot on what had been Jerusalem, or even to gaze on it from afar off. Once again we see Jesus' prophetic insight and foresight. It was the work of a false Messiah, a pretending Christ, which placed the grim coping-stone on the final devastation of Jerusalem and Judaea and on the obliteration of the Jewish nation as a nation.

It is needless to speak of the false teachers which arose within the Church, for every heresy which has troubled the faith had its rise and genesis in the early years of the Church. Jesus' vision of the future for Church and nation came true.

(*d*) The Signs before the End

With the fourth strand in this chapter we come to a different kind of material. We come to the material which is definitely and directly eschatological. This is the material which describes the signs which will precede the end. The most notable thing about this material is that it is not specifically Christian at all; it is Jewish in its pictures and in its thoughts. The Jew looked for the coming of the Day of the Lord, the day when God would intervene directly in history, the day when this present age would be altogether destroyed, and when the new age would come. That period would be preceded by what the Jews called 'the travail of the Messiah', by events which would be the birth-pangs of the new age. This very word is used in our chapter. 'All these are the beginning of sorrows' (Matthew 24.8, Mark 13.8). The phrase is *archē ōdinōn* and *ōdinai* is the word for the pangs of birth. Both in the Old Testament and in the intertestamental literature these signs which precede the end are fully described, and certain of them occur very definitely in this chapter.

(1) Destruction of personal relationships
There were to be wars and rumors of wars (Matthew 24.6, 7); there was to be a disruption of international relationships; there was to be a destruction of personal relationships. This last may well be referred to in Matthew 24.10: They 'shall betray one another and shall hate one another'.

Egyptian will fight with Egyptian, brother with brother, neighbor with neighbor, city with city, kingdom with kingdom (Isaiah 19.2). A tumult from the Lord will be among them, and every man's hand will be against his neighbor (Zechariah 14.13). Brothers will fall in death with one another; a man will slay his sons and his son's sons; from dawn to sunset they will slay each other (Enoch 100.1, 2). There will be divisions one against another, and continual wars in Israel (Testament of Judah 22.1, 2). Friends will attack one another suddenly, and friend will war against friend (4 Ezra 5.9, 6.24). There will be 'quakings of places, tumult of peoples, schemings of nations, confusion of leaders, disquietude of princes' (4 Ezra 9.3). The fullest picture is in the Apocalypse of Baruch 70.3-6: 'And they shall hate one another, and provoke one another to fight, and the mean shall rule over the honorable, and those of low degree shall be extolled above the famous. . . . Then shall confusion fall upon all men, and some of them shall fall in battle, and some of them shall perish in anguish, and some of them shall be destroyed by their own'. The Mishnah (Sotah, ix. 15) describes the signs of the approach of the Messiah: 'The inhabitants of a city go from district to district without finding compassion. The wisdom of the learned is hated, the godly despised, truth is absent. Boys insult old men, old men stand in the presence of children. The son depreciates the father, the daughter rebels against her mother, the daughter-in-law against her mother-in-law. A man's enemies are his house-fellows.'

One of the signs of the end is this dreadful destruction of all personal relationships, this all-pervading hatred and war; and this finds its statement and its echo in our chapter.

(2) The shattered universe

A standard feature of the signs of the end is cosmic upheaval, the shaking and shattering of the world as it is. We find this in Matthew 24.39 (cf. Mark 13.25, Luke 21.25). The time before the end is to be a time of darkness with no brightness, of gloominess and clouds and thick darkness (Amos 5.18-20, Zephaniah 1.15, Joel 2.2). The stars will give no light, the sun will be darkened and the moon will cease to shine (Isaiah 13.10). The moon will be turned into darkness and the sun into blood and the heavens and the earth will shake (Joel 2.30, 31, 3.15, 16). The stars will leave their orbits; the firmament will fall down; there will be a cataract of fire in which creation will become molten chaos; the order of the seasons and of night and day will be destroyed (Enoch 80.4-8; Sibylline Oracles 3.83-89, 796-806; cf. Testament of Levi 4.1, Assumption of Moses 10.4-6).

One of the signs of the end is the shattered universe; and this too finds its statement and its echo in this chapter.

(3) Universalism

It is possible that the preaching to all nations (Matthew 24.14, Mark 13.10) also finds its origin in the apparatus of the Jewish signs which precede the end. It is quite true that often in the apocalyptic literature the Gentiles are destined for destruction or for slavery; but there is a strongly universalist strain in which all the nations are to be gathered in. All nations shall flow to the house of the Lord to learn the ways of the Lord (Isaiah 2.2-4). All the ends of the earth are invited to look to the Lord and to be saved (Isaiah 45.20-22). The feast of the Lord is for all nations (Isaiah 25.6-8). Israel is destined to be a light to the Gentiles, God's salvation to the ends of the earth (Isaiah 49.6, 51.4, 55.5, 56.6-8, 66.19). The heathen will turn and learn God's way, and will confess the emptiness of their worship and will worship the true God (Jeremiah 3.17, 12.15,16, 16.19-21). Men of all countries and languages will learn from the Jews the way of God (Zechariah 14.9). The Son of Man will be a light to the Gentiles (Enoch 48.4, 5). The Gentiles will be multiplied in knowledge and enlightened through the grace of the Lord and sin will come to an end (Testament of Levi 18.5-9). Nations shall come flocking to Jerusalem from the ends of the earth to find God (Psalms of Solomon 17.34, Sibylline Oracles 3.710-723).

It is easy to stress the particularist Jewish attitude of hostility to the Gentiles; but there is a strongly universalist strand of Jewish thought; and this too may well find its echo and its statement in this chapter.

(4) Gathering dispersed Israel

Finally of these regular signs which precede the end there is the ingathering of Israel. This finds its place in our chapter in Matthew 24.31 and in Mark 13.27. It was the great dream that the dispersed people would be reassembled in Jerusalem. God would bring them back, those ready to perish, the outcasts and the exiles, from Assyria and Egypt and Pathros and Cush and Elam and Shinar and Hamath and the isles of the sea (Isaiah 11.11, 27.12, 13). 'O Jerusalem', says the writer of Baruch, 'look about thee toward the east, and behold the joy that cometh unto thee from God. Lo, thy sons come, whom thou sentest away, they come gathered together from the east to the west at the word of the Holy One, rejoicing in the glory of God'

(Baruch 4.36, 37). The greatest of all the visions of the ingathering is in the Psalms of Solomon:

> Stand on the height, O Jerusalem, and behold thy children,
> From the East and the West, gathered together by the Lord;
> From the North they come in the gladness of their God,
> From the isles afar off God hath gathered them.
>
> *(Psalms of Solomon 11.3)*

Even the dead were to be raised up in order to come back.

The ingathering of the dispersed and exiled Jews was one of the dearest of Jewish dreams; and it finds its statement and its echo in our chapter.

So, then, in this chapter there are gathered together four strands of prophecy about the future – the strand which tells of the destruction of Jerusalem, the strand which tells of the persecution and the hatred to come, the strand which tells of the coming of false Messiahs and deceiving teachers, the strand which tells of the signs which precede the end, and this last strand is woven together of threads which are completely Jewish in their color and their significance.

(e) The Second Coming of Jesus

(1) The Facts

It is when we come to the fifth strand of material in this passage that we come to the material which gives to it its peculiar and special interest and importance, for the fifth strand is the strand which contains the material concerning the Parousia, the Second Coming of Jesus Christ. We shall first of all set down what the passage has to say about the Parousia.

(*a*) The Parousia is to be sudden, magnificent and terrifying, at least to the enemies of Christ (Matthew 24.27, 30, Mark 13.26, Luke 17.24, 21.27). It will be like the lightning flash, and it will be in power, in splendor and in glory.

(*b*) It will be a shattering inbreak of God upon the thoughtless (Matthew 24.37-39, Luke 17.26-27). Just as the Flood came upon men and women who were unconcernedly going about the tasks and the pleasures of life, and suddenly involved them in disaster, so the Parousia will confront with eternity those who are never lifting their eyes beyond time.

(*c*) It will be a time of separation (Matthew 24.40, 41, Luke 17.34, 35). One will be taken and the other will be left. The choice of God will be exercised upon men.

(*d*) The time of its coming is utterly unknown, except only to God (Matthew 24.36, Mark 13.32). Not the angels, not even the Son, still less any man, can know the time of the decisive action of God.

(2) The Consequences

Since all this is the case, certain things necessarily follow.

(*a*) The first consequence is not one which this passage actually sets down, but it is a consequence which must be obvious. Speculation as to the time of the Parousia is not only futile, it is actually blasphemous, for a knowledge which is not given even to the Son to possess surely cannot be a knowledge which the mind of man may covet. What is not given to Jesus Christ to know is very certainly not given to men to know.

(*b*) The remaining three consequences are set down in this passage. There is the demand for *endurance* (Matthew 24.13, Mark 13.13, Luke 21.19). It is he who endures to the end who will be saved. The verb which is used for to endure is *hupomenein*, and the noun which is used for *patience* or *endurance* is *hupomonē*. About these words there is a certain untranslatable quality. They do not describe the attitude of the man who resignedly sits down with bowed head and folded hands and passively allows the flood-tide of disaster and trial to flow over him with a dull submissiveness. They describe what has been called 'a masculine constancy under trial'. There is gallantry in them; they describe the spirit which can transmute suffering into glory. The endurance in question is not mere acceptance; it is the endurance which can use even the terrible experiences of life as a means of strengthening, deepening and refining character, and as a means of coming ever nearer and closer to God.

(c) There is the demand for *wisdom in reading the signs of the times* (Matthew 24.32,33, Mark 13.28-39, Luke 21.29-31). The curious feature of the coming of the end both in Jewish and in early Christian thought was the belief that the coming of the end would be sudden and unpredictable, but that at the same time there would be unmistakable signs that it was certainly on the way. The tragedy of life is that men can read the signs of Nature but are blind to the signs of God.

(d) There is the demand for constant *watchfulness* (Matthew 24.42-51, Mark 13.33-37, Luke 21.34-36, 12.35-48). The Christian must be like a servant at all time ready for his master's coming. He must never be like the servant who uses his master's absence to follow out his own nefarious purposes, and is then caught unawares by his master's home-coming. The key-note of the faith of the early Christians was the word 'Watch'.

(3) In this generation

Up to this point the material of this chapter is straightforward enough; we could say that we have a clear enough picture of the Parousia, in so far as any picture of such an event can be clear; but now into this picture there comes the one piece, which as it were, does not fit. As clearly as it can be said, it is said that all these events are to take place within the lifetime of the generation which heard these words spoken. 'This generation shall not pass, till all these things be fulfilled' (Matthew 24.34, Mark 13.30, Luke 21.32). We must clearly examine the teaching of this whole passage on the Second Coming in the light of this saying.

It is significant that this sentence confronts us with a difficulty which is always emerging, when we examine the teaching of the Gospels on the Second Coming. We find this difficulty very early in the Gospel narrative in Matthew's version of events. In Matthew's story, when Jesus despatched the apostles on their first mission, he said: 'Ye shall not have gone over the cities of Israel, till the Son of man be come' (Matthew 10.23). If Jesus said that, we are plainly confronted with two possibilities – either, he was wrong, or, the saying must be interpreted in some other way than at its literal and face value.

We may well find our key to this difficulty by comparing the different versions of the one saying which are contained in the three Gospels. In Matthew 16.28 Jesus is represented as saying 'Verily I say unto you, There be some standing here, which shall not taste of death, till they see the Son of man coming in his kingdom'. In Mark 9.1 the same saying appears as: 'Verily I say unto you, That there be some of them that stand here, which shall not taste of death, till they have seen the kingdom of God come with power'. In Luke 9.27 the same saying appears as: 'But I tell you of a truth, there be some standing here, which shall not taste of death, till they see the kingdom of God'. Here is a case in which we have to make a choice between different versions of the same saying. It is frequently possible in the gospel narrative to explain different versions of the same saying by assuming that Jesus used the same saying on different occasions, as any preacher might and does, and used it in varying forms. But here the occasion is the same occasion. When we examine these three versions of this saying of Jesus, the conclusion is, that if Matthew's version is the correct one, then Jesus' prediction was not fulfilled, and that he was mistaken. But if the version of Mark and Luke is correct, the saying was abundantly fulfilled, because the Kingdom did indeed come with power within the lifetime of many who heard it, for in one generation the message and the power of the gospel did go out from Jerusalem to Samaria, to Judaea and to the uttermost parts of the earth, and the Kingdom did come with power upon men. We may well hold here that a saying which originally spoke of the coming of the Kingdom was personalized into a saying which spoke of the coming of Jesus Christ.

This is part of a larger phenomenon which manifests itself in the Gospels. In the Gospels it is strangely true that there are sayings which seem to be on the face of it foundational evidence for the doctrine of the Second Coming, and which on closer examination will not support the structure of doctrine which has been erected upon them.

The most notable of such sayings is the saying of Jesus at his trial before the High Priest. There are three versions of Jesus' answer to the demand of the High Priest for an answer to the question whether or not He was the Christ, the Son of God. In each case Jesus accepted that claim. In Matthew 26.64 he is represented as going on to say: 'Hereafter shall ye see the Son of man sitting on the right hand of power, and coming in the clouds of heaven'. In Mark 14.62 the same saying runs, 'Ye shall see the Son of man sitting on the right hand of power, and coming in the clouds of heaven'. In Luke 22.69 the saying becomes: 'Hereafter shall the Son of man sit on the right hand of the power of God'. It is clear that, whatever we may conclude in regard to the versions of Matthew and Mark, Luke's version has no reference to the Second Coming whatsoever. It has long since been noted that this saying goes back to a passage in Daniel 7.13,14. In that passage one like unto a son of man comes with the clouds of heaven into the presence of the

ancient of days, and there is given to him a dominion, a glory
and a kingdom, which are universal and eternal. That is to say,
the original passage describes, not an arrival on earth, but an
arrival in heaven. The entire probability, therefore, is that Jesus
was not in this passage foretelling his Second Coming, but he
was saying: 'At the moment you look on me as a criminal in your
power, to do with as you will, to send to a Cross. But the day
will come when you will see me throned in glory with God.'
The exact parallel to this passage will then be Philippians
2.9-11 where it is said that because of Jesus' complete obedience
God has highly exalted him and has given him a name at which
every creature in all the universe will bow in submission. It is a
foretelling, not of his return to earth, but of his enthronement
in the glory of the heavenly places.

The Meaning of the Second Coming
Can we, then, in view of this passage, and in view of the general
teaching in the Gospels, come to any general conclusions about
the meaning of the Parousia of Jesus Christ? It seems that there
are four possible lines of approach.

(a) A definite event in history
We may regard the Parousia of Jesus Christ as one definite event
which will take place at some unknown time in the future. We
may look for the Second Coming of Jesus Christ as an event in
history, even if it is the event to end history. Lines of argument
to support this view are not lacking. It may be said that, so far
as there is an orthodox view of the Second Coming, this is the
orthodox view. It well fits in with the whole Biblical view of
history. It would be the New Testament counterpart, or rather
the New Testament fulfilment, of the Old Testament picture of
the Day of the Lord. In the historical Second Coming of Jesus
Christ the Old Testament expectation of the Day of the Lord

would find its true consummation and completion. It might be well said that the historical Second Coming of Jesus Christ is the essential corollary of his Resurrection and his Ascension and Exaltation. The Resurrection vindicated every claim of Jesus Christ, and the Second Coming would be the universal demonstration of the universal and eternal lordship of Jesus Christ. An historical Second Coming would conserve the great Christian and Biblical truth that history is going somewhere towards a goal, that there is a plan and a purpose in events, that history is not circular and repetitive, not pointless and purposeless, not on the way to slow extinction, but that it has a consummation in the mind of God. It is further to be said that there is little doubt that in the thought of the Early Church the Second Coming was to be an historical event involving the Christians and all mankind. The arguments for the Second Coming as a future, definite event are strong; but nonetheless it remains true that the evidence for this kind of Second Coming is not nearly so strong in the Gospels as at first sight it appears, and it may well be that we shall have to seek some other line of approach.

(*b*) The Holy Spirit is the Second Coming of Jesus
It is possible to argue that the Second Coming of Jesus Christ has happened in the coming of the Holy Spirit. To all intents and purposes this would mean that the events of Pentecost constitute the Second Coming of Jesus Christ. There is at least something of this conception in the thought of the Fourth Gospel. 'I will not leave you comfortless', says the Christ of the Fourth Gospel, 'I will come to you' (John 14.18), and that coming was definitely in the coming of the Holy Spirit. 'If a man love me, he will keep my words: and my Father will love him, and we will come unto him, and make our abode with him' (John 14.23). There is no doubt that the Fourth Gospel does see

the coming of the Spirit as the coming of Jesus Christ into a man's life. This would be in the most literal sense to spiritualize the whole idea of the Second Coming. Jesus Christ would then be the Person who came once in the flesh, and who came again in the Holy Spirit, and who continues so to come.

(*c*) All was completed in Jesus

It is possible to approach the whole conception of the Second Coming along the lines of what is known as realized eschatology. To do that is to say that the whole process of eschatological events has already been realized in Jesus Christ. In him the victory over all evil has finally been won; the powers of darkness and the spirits of evil have finally been defeated. In him the Kingdom has been fully realized and did fully come.

There is a sense in which this is emphatically true. In the life and death of Jesus Christ something did happen to break the power of sin. The Lord's Prayer sets two petitions side by side – 'Thy kingdom come', and 'Thy will be done in earth as it is in heaven'. If we apply the ordinary principles of Hebrew parallelism to these two phrases we may say that the Kingdom of heaven is a society in which God's will is as perfectly done on earth as it is in heaven. And, if that is so, then the Kingdom was fully and finally realized in Jesus Christ, because in him and by him God's will was perfectly done. On this view the Second Coming is no longer a necessary event, because the whole eschatological process and ideal has found its consummation and realization and completion in Jesus Christ.

This idea found its most epigrammatic and succinct expression in the famous dictum that D-day (the day of the allied invasion of Europe) is now past, and V-day (the day of victory) must of necessity follow.

Stated, as it were, in theory there is great attraction in that way of putting things. But one cannot evade the feeling that it does not fit the facts. In point of fact the forces of evil are not subdued, and in point of fact human nature is not changed, and in point of fact sin is not defeated.

The D-day, V-day analogy suffers from one basic defect; the fact is that the process of salvation, God's offer of salvation, the way in which a man is saved, cannot properly be likened to a campaign. When a war has been waged, and when victory has been won, every member of the victorious nation shares in that victory, whether he likes it or not. The nation as a whole is released from danger; the nation as a whole is no longer threatened; the nation as a whole enjoys the benefits of that victory. A man cannot even opt out of that victory; he is a member of a victorious nation. Now the whole point of the benefits of salvation in Christ is that they have to be appropriated. Assuredly man can neither merit them nor achieve them, but he must appropriate them. A much closer analogy is the discovery of some cure whereby a fatal illness can be cured and overcome. Even if there be such a cure, the person suffering from that illness can find no cure until he accepts the cure and submits to the treatment and appropriates the benefits which are now available for him. Christ's victory is a victory which has to be appropriated. We, therefore, suggest that there is still another way in which to approach this whole matter of the Parousia, the Second Coming, of Jesus Christ.

(*d*) Personalized eschatology

There is the way which, we suggest, may be described by the phrase *personalized eschatology*. It is possible to think of the whole eschatological process, and, in particular, of the Second Coming of Jesus Christ, as happening within the individual heart and soul.

The coming of Jesus Christ in the flesh was an event in history. But it is an event which is different from any other event which ever happened in history. It makes no difference to a man's present life in this world or to his eternal welfare in any other world, if he never thinks of, or if he totally disregards, the historical event of the Battle of Hastings. It does not essentially affect him, even if he is quite unaware that that battle was ever fought. No one would ever dream of sending missionaries to the ends of the earth to tell men that William of Normandy landed in Sussex in England in the year 1066. But we do seek to bring the news to all mankind that Jesus Christ was born into Palestine. We do so because we believe that the coming into the world of Jesus Christ was an event which has its direct value for every man.

Now, if a man is unaware of the coming of Christ, he has to be told of it. If he disregards it, he has to be brought to see its supreme importance. And, therefore, it is literally true to say that Jesus Christ has to come again into every individual life. The shattering change, the inbreak of God, the inexplicable arrival of Jesus Christ, the whole eschatological process has to take place within the individual human heart and soul, till Christ comes again into the life of every man, and until eschatology so becomes personalized.

The Parousia of Christ, his Second Coming, is not a subject on which anyone would wish, or indeed has any right, to dogmatize. But it may well be that the whole picture of it in Scripture is a vivid, dramatic, symbolic representation of a process which must take place within the individual human heart, so that the whole eschatological process, and the Second Coming of Christ, become personalized in each man's being.